College Admissions Success

A Counselor's Sure-Fire Guide For High School Students

Ellie Duley

College Admissions Success Copyright © 2017 by Ellie Duley.

All rights reserved. Printed in the United States of America. No part of this book may be used or reproduced in any manner whatsoever without written permission except in the case of brief quotations embodied in critical articles or reviews.

Published by Prominence Publishing.

For information, visit www.prominencepublishing.com

Duley College Counseling, LLC
124 Court St.
Farmington, ME 04938
http://duleycollegecounseling.com

ISBN: 978-0-9958274-4-8

First Edition: April 2017

Table of Contents

A Note for Parents i
Introduction 1
Chapter One: Definition of College 5
    Community Colleges 5
    Public University System 6
    Private Non-Profit 7
    Private For-Profit 8
    A Note About Selectivity 9
Chapter Two: Starting the College Process 11
Chapter Three: Naviance 19
Chapter Four: How to Find Schools to Visit 21
Chapter Five: Testing 25
    PSAT 25
    SAT 26
    ACT 27
    To Prep or Not to Prep? 28
    Test Optional Schools 28
Chapter Six: Major Decisions 31
    Personality Profiles 32
    Interest Inventories 33
Chapter Seven: Finding the Fit 35
    Questions For Parents 35
Chapter Eight: Demonstrated Interest 43
    Visiting 44

  Social Media 44

  Mailing List 44

  Email to Admissions 45

  College Fairs 45

  Email Representative 45

  Meet With Rep at High School 46

Chapter Nine: Road Trip 47

  Pictures 48

  Tour Guides 49

  Explore On Your Own 50

  Talk With Students 50

  College Visit Evaluation Form 51

Chapter Ten: The List 55

Chapter Eleven: Letters of Recommendation 61

  Counselor Letter of Recommendation 61

  Teacher Letters of Recommendation 63

  Other Types of Letters of Recommendation ... 64

Chapter Twelve: The (dreaded) Essay 67

Chapter Thirteen: The "Why College X" Essay 75

Chapter Fourteen: Activities 79

Chapter Fifteen: Application Platforms 87

  The Common Application or Commonapp 87

  SlideRoom 95

  School Specific Applications 95

  Universal Application 97

  Coalition Application 97

  ZeeMee 98

Chapter Sixteen: Dreaded Deadlines 101
    Early Decision (ED) 101
    Early Action (EA) 102
    Regular Decision (RD) 103
    Rolling Admissions (RA) 103
    Restricted Early Action (REA) 103
Chapter Seventeen: Scholarships and Financial Aid 105
    Financial Aid 107
    Need Based Aid 108
    Net Price Calculator 111
    Merit Aid or Money 112
Chapter Eighteen: The Acceptance Letter (and other options) .. 113
Chapter Nineteen: Financial Aid Packages 117
Chapter Twenty: Accepted Students Days 123
Chapter Twenty-One: Honors Colleges and Programs 129
Chapter Twenty-Two: Orientation 133
Chapter Twenty-Three: Getting Ready to Fly 135
Chapter Twenty-Four: You're Here, Now What 141
    Social Media 142
    Opportunities Outside of the Classroom 142
    Go to Class 143
    Time Management 143
    Take Care of Yourself and Others 144
    Resources 145
    Office Hours 145

A Note for Parents

Having a child go away to college is both exciting and heart-wrenching. You've spent so many years getting that child ready to go off into to the world, but even the most self-assured parents and children will have doubts when it comes to leaving the house.

As a trained school counselor, I've dealt with a lot of students and their parents and have seen that anxiety can run high around the whole college process. I remember talking to one first time college mom who told me that she hadn't felt sick to her stomach yet that day. This was in September of her son's senior year of high school. I pictured a year of antacids for this poor mom. In my opinion, she may have been taking on a little too much of the stress, but you can't really control these things sometimes. He was fine, by the way.

I remember reading everything that I could find when my first son was going through high school and talking about college. I wanted to make sure that he was taking the right classes and doing all the right things. I remember that he was invited to apply for the National Honor Society during his junior year. It was a big deal in his school and for the kids who shared similar classes and GPAs, but he wasn't particularly interested. I made him fill out the application, write the essay and eventually join the club. I don't know what he really got out of being a member of NHS, but I remember it being so important to me that he join. Something sounds wrong here, right? We all want what's best for our kids and I wanted him to have as many advantages as possible when it came to college applications. He is in his mid-twenties now and I'm just starting to hear the, "You were right, mom," comments. Not about NHS-that one might not come until he is a parent and wanting what's best for his own child. It might never come at all.

This book is designed as a handbook for the college going student. It's perfectly fine for parents to read it, but frankly, there is a lot in here that might not be of interest (except for financial aid because everyone is interested in that!). You might find some interesting info at the end of the book: after the work of applying is done. You may see the family dynamics are changing, even before your child leaves for school and this is perfectly normal and more on that at the end of the book.

In my private practice, I meet with the family (or at least one parent) first. I like to see what I can about family dynamics and I like for parents to have a chance to ask questions before we get started. It's a good time to assess our fit both from the student's side and mine as well. I have some families where parents are very involved and like to come to all meetings. I do prefer to do essay brainstorming without parents because I like kids to feel free to say whatever they may be thinking, but I've had parents sit in on these meetings. It's rare and I've only had to rein in the parents one or two times for doing all the talking. Basically, I just want everyone to be comfortable with the process. I will often tell students to go home and talk with their parents about the essay brainstorming that we do. Parents can have a lot of good input and are the experts on their child. I have parents who stay in close touch with me via email and others who I never hear from unless I reach out with a question. I like to help empower the students to take ownership of their college application process by gently guiding them along the way and providing small assignments to encourage self-reflection.

I'm still a certified school counselor and consider the code of ethics that come with my degree to be the best for my practice as well as being true to my beliefs. I am also a member of several national and local organizations and follow their ethics codes as well. I tell students and families that I will only disclose what students tell me in confidence if there is a danger to the child or others, but this work isn't like the work that I did in a school counseling office and I've never had to break confidentiality. In fact, students don't really disclose much that isn't pertinent to the job at hand.

I love when students ask for meetings to go over what we are working on or to talk about college visits and tours, but I will ask for meetings with students who haven't been in touch. I know how busy students are so I do my best to work around their schedules and anticipate needs. Sometimes, I will text a student and ask for a casual meeting just because I haven't seen them in a while and I want to get my eyes on them to see how they are holding up. This is generally reserved for seniors in the throes of things. Students can meet with me every week if they'd like, but most are too busy. I will reach out when I know deadlines are looming to make sure that we are on the same page and have plenty of time to get those essays checked for content and grammar. It's ridiculous how excited I get when I receive an email or text that a student has been accepted to a school and earned a nice scholarship or has gotten great SAT or ACT scores.

I tell my families that the best thing that parents can do is support their student through the process. I like for students to take the lead by signing up for tours and info sessions, but they will need to talk with parents about the logistics of getting to the schools and any overnight accommodation needs that might come up with a multi-day college tour. Signing up for tours is so easy now-you don't even need to make a phone call! I also advise both parents and students to attend all parent nights that their high school puts on regarding college and financial aid.

The whole college process is very individualized and this is also true with my practice. It's very important to me that everyone's needs are met during this exciting time.

Introduction

You've probably picked up this book because you are thinking of and/or planning to go to college, or you are the parent of someone who you think may want to go to college at some point.

First, I'll start with a bit about me and how I came into this work. I started a master's degree program in school counseling while my kids were still living at home. My youngest has autism so I had many years staying at home coordinating his care and negotiating with two different school systems. While this certainly felt like my life's work and a worthy use of my time, I also had time to think about what I'd like to do, career-wise, when the kids were grown.

After earning my master's I worked in local school districts as a high school counselor. This is very rewarding work and I loved the hustle and bustle of working in a high school, but there are three domains in the school counseling world. According to the American School Counselors Association (ASCA), counselors should divide their time between counseling academics, career, and social and emotional health. I always felt that I never had enough time in the career domain, which covers all aspects of post-secondary planning including college. It was because of this that I took the plunge and opened an Independent Educational Consultant (IEC) practice. I am typically, hired by parents, but most of the work that I do is directly with the student. I work with students beginning as early as the end of eighth grade and sometimes as late as senior year.

I begin my work by doing a transcript review, which ensures that the student is on track to graduate and that there will be no surprises senior year when, for whatever reason, the student doesn't have enough fine arts credits or whatever the problem might be. Virtually every school district has different graduation requirements so I have developed forms for individual schools and can quickly see if a student is missing anything.

I also go over course selection to make sure that students are taking the most appropriate courses to meet their educational goals. You will read much more about this later. I strategize with the student on college admission testing and, eventually, work with the student to build a college list. I advise on college visits and help the student brainstorm for college essays.

One of the biggest benefits to working outside the school system is that I have time to read and learn about new trends in college admissions. I also visit an average of 30 colleges and universities each year so I can give an up to date perspective on what's happening on college campuses. I attend several conferences and have the opportunities to talk with admissions representatives about what's new in the college admission world. Two things that I don't do are writing the essay or guaranteeing admission to specific institutions.

I belong to several national and local organizations with other IECs and admissions professionals. I am a professional member in the Independent Educational Consultants Association, (IECA) as well as a member in the National Association for College Admission Counseling, (NACAC), and the New England Association for College Admission Counseling, (NEACAC). I attend at least two professional conferences a year and keep in close touch with admissions professionals, school counselors and other IECs.

This book is a handbook filled with advice and worksheets that I use with my students and families. It can be seen as a, "What happens when" guide during the admissions process and beginning as early as eighth grade. I discovered while working in different high schools that college really is my passion. It was frustrating to me that I didn't have more time to devote to the whole college process. I love visiting different campuses and seeing the students as they navigate their way around that special time between high school and leaving the family home for good. I consider myself a college geek and I'm OK with that!

I've worked with many different families and for many different reasons. I've worked with families where neither parent had attended college and the parents felt that this was too important a decision to 'wing it' or go it alone.

I can tell you that college admissions has changed significantly since my older son attended the University of Connecticut in 2008. In less than ten years the college landscape has changed with the addition of new application platforms and the redesign of admission tests. It's confusing and overwhelming at best. Some families just don't have the time to learn about the college process and keep up with all the changes and would rather employ an IEC to keep them on track.

I've also worked with families who, with great insight into their children, wanted to keep peace at home. I tell moms that I will do the nagging for them, but I've also found that with my specific timeline and gentle nudges along the way, that I really don't have to do too much nagging. I know that it's always easier for kids to hear something from a third person. I've certainly seen it with my own kids! A few years ago I took an hourly job helping a student with her essay. We looked at the question together and talked about her thoughts.

Together we put together a rough outline. The girl is an excellent writer, but she didn't want her mom to help her with the organization and collection of her thoughts. I spent about an hour with her and another hour suggesting revisions and we were done. Mom was happy because it was one week before the deadline and the nagging stopped immediately. I've only met this student that one time, but I've kept in touch with her mom occasionally and the reports are that the student is very happy at her first choice school.

Everything about applying to college is individualized. From when to test and which tests to take, to class selection, and eventually, the college list. It is different for each student. For this reason, this book is designed with the assumption that the student will have access to help along the way. I've outlined what your student should be thinking about and when he should be thinking about it, but it would certainly be helpful to have someone on hand for guidance. I've added questions to the end of every chapter that may be worth investigating.

This could be someone like me, an IEC, or it could be a school counselor. I always recommend that students get to know their counselors early and often, but counselors are often torn in several directions with additional responsibilities such as testing and increasing mental health counseling. I think that this is the main reason that so many families use the services of IEC's. I am only one of thousands of consultants in the United States. There are also many who work internationally. It's a growing business and invaluable service to families and students.

So, with all this in mind, let's looks at "What happens when", keeping in mind that there are often several things happening at once.

Chapter One

Definition of College

Many high schools define college rather loosely. It can often be any kind of post-secondary training such as a certificate, associate's degree, military service or a four-year bachelor's degree. First, I will break down the different options and then for the rest of the book I will concentrate on what you would want to know if you, (or someone you love), is planning to attend a four-year college or university with the end goal of obtaining a bachelor's degree.

Community Colleges

Community colleges are all about access. They accept most people who apply, although certain programs are more competitive and thus harder to get into or have waitlists. To be accepted into a community college you will most likely need a high school diploma, General Equivalency Diploma, (GED) or HiSET, (the test that's replaced the GED) test. That's all. You may have to take a placement test. The ACCUPLACER, which is usually offered right at the college, is much shorter than the SAT, which may also be used for placement if you've taken that test recently. The ACCUPLACER or SAT will determine if you need to take a course or two to get up to speed. These developmental courses are typically not for credit and won't count toward a degree, but some schools will allow them as electives so this is something you should ask about.

Community colleges are also, typically, a lot more affordable than traditional four-year colleges and universities. For this reason, some students plan to do two years at a community college and transfer into a four-year institution. This is a good way to graduate with little or no debt, but a word of caution if this is your plan. Make sure to let the community college know your intentions early on in the process. They will help you select courses that will transfer and be credited to your eventual degree.

Community colleges offer both certificates (usually a one year program) and associate's degrees, which typically take two years to complete for full-time students.

Some community colleges have dorms and sports teams, which offer a more typical college experience for students who want to complete a program that is shorter than a bachelor's degree. There are lots of options with community colleges. In Maine, for example, the seven community colleges reach all corners of the state and offer over 160 degrees and certificates.

Public University System

Every state in the country has a public university system. These systems usually have one flagship university, which is the main school and often the biggest school in the system. The flagship university will offer many different colleges under the umbrella of the university-for example there might be a college of business, college of arts and sciences, college of engineering, etc.

The public university system receives some funding from the state, although, this is becoming less and less in many states. Because they receive state funding, these schools are less expensive for in-state students as opposed to out-of-state students. They can often be the most affordable way to get a four-year degree without dealing with transferring from a community college, but not always! Check out the next section to understand how this could be.

There are some flagship schools that offer reciprocity agreements with other states and under these circumstances tuition may be somewhere in between in-state and out-of-state prices. This deal may be specific to major or just an agreement between states.

There are usually other, smaller, state schools in the system that may specialize in certain fields or offer university access to other parts of the state. State flagstaff universities often offer advanced degrees and doctoral programs where the smaller state universities may not.

Some flagship universities are considered to offer such a phenomenal education that they are considered 'public Ivies' like the University of Virginia, the University of Vermont and the University of Michigan in Ann Arbor. This designation also makes them much more selective than other state universities. Obtaining admission is much harder and merit money, money granted to students based on talents or achievements, is less available or spread among more students. The University of North Carolina at Chapel Hill is capped at accepting no more than 18% of each incoming class from out-of-state. This makes admission for out-of-state students very selective, especially if the student isn't an athlete. Many students will use their in-state flagship university as both an academic and financial safety school. For this reason, alone, it is worth a tour to your state school.

Private Non-Profit

Private non-profit schools come in a wide range of shapes and sizes. They are the Ivies, the small liberal arts colleges that have a long history in this country, the career based colleges that train students for careers in business and other careers like law enforcement, and schools that combine liberal arts with engineering. Basically, there is a private non-profit school for whatever academic course in which your interest lies.

These private non-profits tend to charge a lot more in tuition than the public universities, but they also may offer more in the way of financial aid.

Speaking of financial aid, there are two basic types that need to be considered: need based and merit aid. Need based financial aid is just what it sounds like. It is calculated based on a family's ability to pay for college (see more about this in the financial aid section) and merit money is awarded for a students achievements in the classroom and sometimes on the playing field, theater stage or debate team, (as well as other institutional priorities-or what individual colleges might be looking for at any given time).

Private non-profits usually have a pretty high sticker price, which can often send families into college sticker shock, but often will discount the price at least a bit. In fact, it is a good idea to get an idea of what the discount rate is at any of the private non-profits though this information is not always readily available. Private non-profits are being run more like a business, which essentially they are. Some will discount up to 50% of the tuition and others keep their tuition lower and pride themselves on not having a large tuition discount rate. This is where doing your research will really pay off (pun intended). It is also where the Net Price Calculator can come into play-see chapter 17.

Private For-Profit

Private for-profits have seen a lot of scrutiny and a bit of controversy lately. These schools are very inclusive and accept the majority of students who apply. They often offer a majority of their courses online and appeal to the non-traditional college student; a student who is already working and looking to make a career change or wants to get additional training to get to the next level of his/her career.

Most are accredited to receive federal student aid and use the same form that the non-profit colleges and universities use, which is the Free Application for Federal Student Aid, (the FAFSA).

The private for-profit college is not the typical path for a student coming out of high school, but there are certain programs that are attractive to high school and older students alike. If you are interested in a private for-profit school you need to know that they are definitely run on a business model and profits are very important. This doesn't mean that they offer little value to college-going students', it just means that students should evaluate the program carefully and make sure that it fits their needs.

It is important when looking at all schools to consider the graduation rates and dig deeper if it looks like students aren't able to graduate in a four to six year time frame. Are required classes not offered every semester? Are required classes only offered at inconvenient times? There are lots of reasons for graduation to be delayed, but every semester spent in college is a semester spent not working and gaining experience in a student's chosen field.

When doing college research, no matter what type of school you are looking at, you should always check the college and what accreditations they hold for the program that you are interested in. This can be the difference between getting a job and being passed over for someone who graduated with necessary accreditation.

A Note About Selectivity

Selectivity is basically the percentage of students who apply and who are admitted. Highly selective schools, like the Ivies, may only accept ten percent or fewer of the students who apply and some public universities may accept up to 90% of students. You can see that there is a huge difference between the two. The more selective colleges will also probably have more requirements for admission and even a more intensive application for admission.

Most four-year colleges and universities like to see two years of a foreign language, but most highly selective schools like to see four years of a foreign language-preferably the same language. This is important information during your sophomore year of high school when you may be having that, "Can I drop French?" conversation with your parents. The answer is probably yes, but are you willing to close some doors? There will be more about this in the high school preparation section.

Highly selective schools also look for students who have challenged themselves with the most rigorous classes (referred to as rigor in the college admission world), taken leadership roles in clubs and sports in high school and may be involved in volunteering outside of school. Selectivity is just one of the factors that you will look at and think about when making your college list.

I will present some questions to ponder (or ask someone about) that will help you on your journey toward finding the college that is your best academic, social and financial fit at the end of each chapter. These questions may be more appropriate at different times in your process. You don't have to have these questions answered, but it might help make the process more clear as well as opening up dialog surrounding the whole college process.

Questions dealing with selectivity might be:

1. With which level am I am best lined up?
2. Which colleges in my state are private non-private?
3. Does more than one community college offer culinary (or any major in which you may be interested)?

Chapter Two

Starting the College Process

As a former public school counselor and now an Independent Educational Consultant (IEC), I am often asked when is the best time to start thinking about college. I have a couple thoughts about this. For parents, I would say the best time to start thinking about college is when your children are young and you can begin to save for this very large expense. Google "529 plans" in your state for specific college savings offered in your state or see a financial advisor for other plans and the tax benefits that they carry. For students, I say that the best time is when you are ready to think about your future.

As a counselor, I like to begin working with students either at the end of eighth grade, yes, I did just say eighth grade, or during the ninth grade year before classes are selected for sophomore year.

As I mentioned earlier, I'm all about leaving as many doors open when thinking about post-secondary (four-year college, for the sake of this book) as possible. I obviously don't spend as much time with my freshmen as I do my seniors, who are in the throes of college applications from the end of junior year until usually the end of December.

What I can do for my younger students is advise them on class selection such as the foreign language example I spoke of earlier. I also touch base with these students at least at the end of every semester and can help catch any downward trends or help a struggling student get back on track. I'm very informal about this and will react to a situation if a parent calls to report that their child is struggling. It may be as simple as coaching a student on how to approach a teacher for extra help, or it may be helping the family find a tutor to help the student with a specific class. The student's school counselor can also provide academic coaching and I advise clients to get to know their school counselor early because it's very important in the college process. Counselors are the ones who write letters of recommendation and release transcripts to colleges. It's best for you to make an appointment with your counselor to have post-secondary option conversations early and often.

Course selection conversations are a great opportunity for me to check in with students to see if their thoughts about their future have changed at all. I believe that all students should take the classes that most challenge them without overwhelming them. Here are some examples of situations that benefit from a conversation before class selection time in the spring:

- ❖ I am often asked by parents if a student would be better off taking an Advanced Placement (AP) class and getting a B or taking an honors level class and getting an A. Colleges are also asked this question and I've often heard admission representatives from highly selective institutions say that students should take the AP and get an A. This is always followed by nervous laughter. My answer is probably going to be to go with the honors class, by the way, but I would certainly want to see the students schedule and transcript before making that call.

- ❖ I also believe that potentially college-bound students should take foreign language for at least the first two years, if at all possible.

❖ Another thing that I like to see students do is to get a lot of the graduation requirements out of the way in the first two years of high school. This keeps the door open if a student would like to explore vocational technical opportunities that require several class periods per week. I hate to see when a student who really wants to learn culinary, for example, but can't take the class because if he does then he won't have time to fulfill graduation requirements like health, PE or fine arts. Students can get into this bind by failing classes and having to spend time retaking them, or by taking a bunch of electives early on that don't fulfill graduation requirements. Getting required classes out of the way also opens up the option for students to take classes at local colleges or community colleges. This could lead to the student entering college with college credit and it's usually much more affordable as many high schools and colleges have agreements for high school students who are interested in taking college classes.

❖ Occasionally, there are students who will double up on math during their sophomore year, taking both algebra II and geometry. This might be appropriate for a student who wasn't placed into an advanced math course earlier in school, but is showing math proficiency and ability in high school and would like to be able to take math through calculus in high school. Having calc already under your belt in high school can make you more attractive to colleges and might be important for some calculus based majors when looking at colleges.

Those examples illustrate why I like to start working with students earlier rather than in the fall of senior year. This is my perfect world scenario and I don't charge families more if we start working together earlier, but what often happens is that I'm often called in to consult when the student is in her junior or even senior year. This is fine, but, as I mentioned before, she may have fewer choices due to doors being closed earlier in her high school years.

There are other reasons why I like to meet with students and their families early on during the high school years. The PSAT test is offered in October every year. It's very common for sophomores to take this test and some states use the test as a state assessment so students may not have a choice in the matter. It's also common for juniors to take the test, but it might be seen as more optional in some high schools. This is a shame as it is a test that could lead to scholarships later on if the student does really well, (only juniors are considered for the National Merit Scholarship).

Besides the PSAT, I like to have a conversation regarding other college admission tests. I like to outline a testing schedule so that students aren't overwhelmed with testing at the end of junior year and during the beginning of senior year.

If a student is taking AP or honors classes and is already thinking that he might like to apply to highly selective schools or the Ivies then I might suggest taking a subject test in that class at the end of sophomore year when the information is fresh. It's always a case-by-case situation. 2016 was particularly challenging due to the redesign of the SAT. Some of my clients moved over to the ACT while others took the new SAT a few times-again, case-by-case.

Here is a convenient place to keep track of all your scores:

CollegeBoard tests:

PSAT (10th) Total_____EBRW_____Math_____

PSAT (11th) Total_____EBRW_____Math_____

SAT

Date_____Total_____EBRW_____Math_____
Date_____Total_____EBRW_____Math_____
Date_____Total_____EBRW_____Math_____

SAT Subject tests (please list subject, score and date taken):

1.

2.

3.

Another option for college admission testing:

ACT

Date_____Composite_____Math_____Science_____
_____STEM_____
English_____Reading_____Writing (optional)_____

Date_____Composite_____Math_____Science_____
_____STEM_____
English_____Reading_____Writing (optional)_____

Tests for potential college credit:

AP

Please list courses and scores:

1.   4.

2.   5.

3.   6.

Please list any college classes that you've taken:

1.

2.

3.

While you are listing your test scores you may as well have a place to put your academic distinctions as you will need to list them on your college application. These can be book awards that are usually handed out at the end of junior year in a school assembly or department awards within your school.

1.

2.

3.

4.

    College tours are another reason to start the college process before junior year. If you have absolutely no idea where you would like to attend college then sophomore year is a great time to get out a see a bunch of different types of schools. This is just to get a feel for the different options-big city schools or small liberal arts colleges that are in out-of-the-way locations? These things need to be sorted out. I think it's really important to tour when students are on campus, but initial tours can be done in the summer if you've planned a family vacation near a campus that might be of interest.

Other than touring and testing during sophomore year, the best thing that you can do is do well in all classes. If a you look at high school like it's your day job and always turn in your best work it will set you up with more options when it's time to get serious about the college search.

Another thing to pay attention to is your attendance! Many schools will penalize you for too many unexcused absences, by docking your grade. These are not days where you are truly sick, but more like days that you just aren't feeling school or days when you decide that a powder day on the slopes is better than physics. Hey, I think so, too, but you still need to go to school.

I've seen attendance listed on transcripts and colleges will, too. If your algebra II grade is a C- and you've missed 19 classes in one semester then the obvious conclusions to be drawn will not be in your favor.

Schoolwork and classes aren't the only things that you should be paying attention to in high school. Most high schools have a variety of clubs and student run organizations. It's important to join a club or two and maybe play a sport or two because these are the places where you will meet your friends, plus, they are fun, which is a nice balance to academics. It is also where you can gain leadership experience and learn other important skills. Ideally, I'd like to see you get involved in your high school community during your freshman year. It may be that the first club that you join isn't what you were looking for and this is fine. You will learn from the experience of trying something new even if it isn't something that you stick with. Having said that, it's nice to spend a few years with a club or sport and try different roles within that activity over the course of time.

I get asked a lot about volunteering because people think that colleges want to see this—and they do. I had a client come to see me with her mom in October of her senior year and ask about volunteering. She was a varsity athlete and overwhelmed with the college application process. They were both very relieved when I said to forget about volunteering. Why would I say this? Colleges like to see volunteer work, but it should be something that the student is passionate about and, ideally, it should be sustained over a period of time. Volunteering just to have something to put on a college application is probably a waste of everyone's time—especially in the fall of senior year when you are already really busy and overwhelmed. If you have an interest and have time to give back to your community, then by all means do so. My personal feeling is that giving back to your community can be very fulfilling and something that everyone should do when they can. Helping others helps everyone. You can also learn something about yourself in the process. Helping to coach a team of five-year-old soccer players may help you to decide that going into elementary education may not be your cup of tea, or it could be the best couple of hours of your week!

1. Are my PSAT scores any good?
2. When should I take the SAT or ACT?
3. Do you know where I can find volunteer opportunities?

Chapter Three

Naviance

Some high schools use a software program called Naviance. This tool helps students' research careers and matches them with colleges that could be a good fit. This is often a good place to start if your district has this resource. Often it will be purchased by a school district and students will have access to the software from as young as Kindergarten. Students will have to fill out a profile, but this may often be done in advisory or in a class.

The software will walk you through the college search process and give you tools similar to the ones I present in this book to help get you ready to meet your goals.

This is just a tool to use in high school to help with the college process and is not a college application platform like the ones that I will discuss later.

If your school doesn't have Naviance your college application process will not be any different than students with access to this software. The only difference might be how you craft your list.

I've not worked in a district that has Naviance, but as an independent counselor I've worked with students who have access to Naviance and students who don't. The process that I use is exactly the same so don't worry if you don't have this tool. If you do have access to this tool, then by all means use it for career and college research.

Naviance has a resume template, but most college applicants won't need a resume unless they have a large number of really great activities or if the college specifically asks for one.

Interestingly, it seems that students with access to Naviance seem to hire private consultants at a higher rate than students without the software. I assume this has to do with the culture of the towns that can afford the software or other demographical differences.

1. Am I at a disadvantage if my school doesn't have Naviance?
2. Is there another program that will give me the same information?

Chapter Four

How to Find Schools to Visit

With almost 4000 colleges and universities in the country it can be hard to figure out where to start when thinking about places to visit. I already mentioned looking at a college or two if there is one nearby a place that you might be visiting. If you live in Florida and Gram and Gramps live in Ohio you just might have an opportunity to poke around some colleges in the Midwest.

College fairs are a great way to gain access to a large number of colleges in one place. Check with the school counseling office to see if there is a college fair coming to a town near you-your school may even be sending a bus that you can sign up for if you want to go during the school day. Most of the big fairs are offered twice: once during the school day and again at night so you don't have to miss class. You can probably get the list of schools of who will be attending in advance so you can even do some research on different colleges before you attend. Be prepared because college fairs can be crowded with students and families.

Colleges each have table with promotional materials and an admissions representative will be nearby to answer any questions you might have about the college. Speaking of questions, it's a good idea to go with a list. Some things you might like to ask are:

- How many undergraduate students attend your school?
- What play is your drama department working on currently?
- Is there an opportunity for undergraduates to conduct research?
- Do teacher's assistants (TA's) teach classes or do professors?
- What is the average class size for introductory classes?
- Does the college provide transportation to the nearest airport before and after breaks? This obviously only applies if you would be taking a plane home for breaks.
- What is the ratio between male and female students?
- Do you have a fencing team (or anything else that is of interest to you)?
- How is the financial aid? Do you offer merit money and if so, what is the average amount?
- How safe is campus?
- Is campus LGBTQ friendly?

These are just a few suggestions and you can ask about a number of things. Often you can use questions to get a conversation started, which might bring up points that you hadn't even thought of yet.

A couple of years ago, I attended a college fair during the day. There were lots of students from local high schools and the room was packed. After the fair I came home and wrote a blog post and came up with a list of college fair do's and don'ts for students when attending fairs. I believe that this advice is still very relevant:

- *Don't clump in a group with your friends. Really, don't, it's hard for others to get around you.*
- *Don't hide in the bathroom.*

- *Put your phone away.*
- *Do get a list of schools if you don't already have one and a map if one is available. Also, grab a bag for college promotional materials.*
- *If you made a list of schools that you'd like to connect with then make sure to seek out these admission reps. If they are busy then move on and circle back before you leave.*
- *Introduce yourself, shake hands and look the rep in the eye. This is good practice for life. It's also polite.*
- *Fill out info forms only for schools that you'd like to receive mail from. Trust me, you will get a lot of mail so you don't need to fill out forms for every school in the room! This is a way to demonstrate your interest to the school.*
- *Take materials from schools that interest you. Again, you don't need to grab something from everyone-it will just overwhelm you later.*
- *Take a business card from the rep if you are very interested in that school and think you might like to apply.*
- *Thank the representative and move along when you've had your questions answered.*

So, college fairs are obviously a good place to learn about different schools, but there are other sources for this information. Talk to friends who may have older siblings to find out where they go to school and how they like it. Your parents might also have a few thoughts about schools that would be a good fit for you and worth a visit. There are also quite a few search engines that you can use to bring up schools that have what you are interested in, whether it be academics, athletics or a certain club. I like the BigFuture search that can be found on the CollegeBoard site at www.bigfuture.collegeboard.org.

1. Can I visit the school in the next town?
2. How do I sign up for a visit?

Chapter Five

Testing

College admissions testing has been around forever. In the past it seemed that the country was divided with students living in the East taking the SAT and students in the Midwest and West taking the ACT. Now it seems like both tests are accepted almost everywhere and some schools have gone test-optional, but more about that later. Both the SAT and the ACT are standardized tests used by colleges to gauge college readiness.

PSAT

The PSAT isn't used for college admission, but it is considered practice for the SAT and is also considered as a tool to measure college readiness for students in 10th and 11th grade. Basically, CollegeBoard, the company that owns the PSAT, SAT, AP and other tests and a financial aid form called the CSS Profile, sets a benchmark for college readiness that students and high schools can use for studying or improving curriculum. The PSAT is offered twice a year, but most high schools offer it in October. The test is for 10th and 11th graders. Some states use the PSAT as an assessment for 10th graders and in this case all students in 10th grade are required to take the test. Students in 11th grade should take the test as another practice if they plan to take the SAT, which typically happens in the spring of junior year. The top juniors will be entered into the National Merit Scholarship Competition (NMSC). This is a really big deal.

It's hard to say who will be entered into the NMSC because it's always the top 50,000 scorers. From here 34,000 students will be given commended students status and the very top 16,000 (this is broken down by state so that every state will have at least someone in this category) move on as NMSC semi-finalists. These semi-finalists are notified through their high school and an application to proceed needs to be completed. The process goes on until scholarship winners are announced. Even if students don't make it past being a commended student or semi-finalist it's the recognition by NMSC that attracts the attention of colleges.

SAT

The SAT, once known as the Scholastic Aptitude Test, is used in some states as a state assessment. This means that you may end up taking this test in school-usually in April of your junior year. The SAT was redesigned in 2016 and caused all sorts of stress, worry, and confusion, but really only for the high school class graduating in 2017. Students graduating from high school after 2017 will probably never know anything different.

This new test is scored on a 1600-point scale and an optional essay is scored separately. The test takes three hours with an additional 50 minutes if you take the essay. You will receive a total score that combines Evidence Based Reading and Writing (EBRW) combined with your Math score. Both sections are scored from 200-800 total points. Your EBRW score is the combination of a reading test and a writing and language test. The math test has two parts-one where you can use a calculator and one where you can't. The math that is on the test ranges from algebra, geometry, trigonometry, data analysis and more. More information and practice questions can be found at the CollegeBoard, (www.collegeboard.org) website.

You can link with Khan Academy, (www.khanacademy.org) for a free and personalized practice plan based on your PSAT results. You will need your test results to get a personalized study guide based on questions and sections that you did poorly on. Since the redesign of the test in 2016 there is no longer a penalty for guessing on answers.

ACT

The ACT is another test that is used for college admissions. The ACT covers a lot of the same information as the SAT, but the scoring is very different. With the ACT you will get a composite score as well as sub-scores in math, science, STEM, reading and English. There is also an optional writing section on the ACT. It's wise to check with colleges that you are interested in to see if they will require either the SAT or ACT essays. More information on the test can be found at the ACT website, www.act.org.

So, what is the difference between tests and who should take which one? After the SAT redesign in 2016 the tests have become quite similar. The SAT gives you a bit more time per question so this might be a consideration if you like more time to think about each question. The test prep companies out there suggest taking a full-length practice test of each (be sure to time it!) and see which feels better. It's hard to compare the scores, but after the redesign, the SAT came up with concordance tables to compare the SAT with the ACT. The ACT, however, does not agree with these tables. Welcome to the confusing world of college admissions testing.

To Prep or Not to Prep?

Test prep is a huge industry in this country (and internationally) and I always get questions about its worth. Basically, the more familiar you are with the test the better you are apt to do on the test.

You can prep on your own with resources from the test websites. Some are free and others you will have to pay for. With independent test prep it really depends on your need for structure and support. The SAT partnership with Khan Academy has opened up a lot more free resources for students to prep on their own for free. The 'on their own' part is the key here. Students have to have the discipline and time management skills to prep on their own.

I have an online test prep software program that is available to my students and I find that many are just not that interested in taking the time to use it correctly. I usually suggest that they at least use it for the free practice tests for both the SAT and ACT.

There are also test prep classes that can run $1,000 or more for an eight-week course. You will spend a few hours a week in a class with other students learning tips, tricks and taking practice tests. I have seen scores go up with test prep, but it's really about what the student is willing to put into it. As with so many things in the college application process the answer to the test prep question is-it depends.

Test Optional Schools

Test optional schools are becoming more and more prevalent especially since the big test companies are changing (both the SAT and the ACT have undergone redesigns lately). Some schools believe that test scores aren't that great a predictor of college success so they don't require or look at them. Other schools believe this to be true as well, but they would like to see something in place of test scores.

Brandeis, for example, has this policy taken from the Brandeis website:

Option 1: Submit SAT or ACT

Option 2: Submit three exams from the approved list. One exam must be from a Science or Math discipline, one exam must be from an English or Social Science discipline, and the third exam may be from a discipline of the student's choice.

Option 3: Submit an academic portfolio through the Common Application or Brandeis Application, including:

"One graded analytical writing sample* from 11th or 12th grade, including the grades and comments for the paper. Examples of acceptable writing samples include expository writing, essay exams, or research papers. We cannot accept creative writing.

One additional recommendation written by an academic teacher from an 11th or 12th grade course."

This leaves it in your hands to choose how to best present your application. For comparison, the most recent information is the 2015-16 application year when Brandeis required the SAT or ACT for admission. Almost 30% of admitted students scored over 700 in critical reading on the OLD SAT and over 50% scored over 700 in math on the same test. These scores are incredibly good.

Other schools will not ask for any additional information when students decide to apply without their test scores, but you will most likely have to take a placement test later if you decide to enroll. It's not usually a big deal, but it is good to know.

1. If I want to do test prep do you have a good program for me?
2. What might be some good test optional schools for me?

Chapter Six

Major Decisions

In my practice, I find that my students and, even more so, my parents are pretty concerned with what you should pick for a college major. It's pretty easy for kids who want to be engineers, nurses or teachers, but students who have no idea what they want to do when they graduate from college struggle when talking about declaring a major.

As it turns out, most liberal arts colleges don't require that students declare a major right away. In fact, at some schools you don't need to declare until after sophomore year. Many schools have academic advisors trained to help undecided students find their path. These advisors will then pass the students along to an advisor within the discipline they choose. It's also true that some students will change majors several times over the course of their college education.

There is a lot of free information on the Internet that can help you try to figure out both what you might be interested in, (interest inventories) and what personality type you are, (personality profiles). I will often use one or both if a student (or parent) really wants to dig and come up with a possible major, which can be helpful when creating a college list, but not necessary.

Personality Profiles

Personality tests are fun and usually pretty quick. The one that I use most often is from the website www.16personalities.com. It's free and can be completed in about 15 minutes. At the end of the test you will be given a personality code that is based on the theory of Carl Jung and the work done around personality types done by Katherine Cook Briggs and her daughter Isabelle Myers. Katherine and Isabelle created the Myers-Briggs Indicator ™, which you may be familiar with. Interestingly, when I went to college Myers-Briggs was used to match roommates, but I digress. At the end of the 16 Personalities test you will get a five-letter code. Below is a quick cheat sheet for the codes, but you can get more detailed information on the website.

Mind indicates how you interact with other people.
- **Introverts** (I)-recharge their batteries by having some alone time and can get exhausted by social interaction.
- **Extroverts** (E)-are energized by social interaction and often seek out others.

Energy indicates how you see the world and how you process information.
- **Intuitive** (N)-if you are this type you may be more curious and open-minded.
- **Observant** (S)-this indicates a tendency to be highly practical.

Nature focuses on how you cope with emotions and how you make decisions.
- **Thinking** (T)-individuals with a T might focus more on rationality over emotion.

- **Feeling** (F)-tend to be emotionally expressive and sensitive.

Tactics looks at your approach to work, planning and decision-making.
- **Judging** (J)-often prefer structure and are highly organized and decisive.
- **Prospecting** (P)-tend to be more flexible and good at improvising.

Identity identifies how confident we are in our abilities and decisions.
- **Assertive** (A)-self-assured and even tempered, this type may have less stress and be less goal driven.
- **Turbulent** (T)-self-conscious and sensitive to stress, turbulent identities may be perfectionists and driven to succeed.

One thing to keep in mind with this and other personality tests and interest inventories—rarely is someone 100% of any type, but rather a mix. These tests look to see which traits are strongest. Also, the outcome is only as good as the information that you input. Read the instructions and be honest. There are no wrong answers with this test!

Interest Inventories

Interest inventories are another tool that can be helpful. These tests look at different things that you might like to do such as cabinet-making, book-keeping and dozens of other things. There are different tasks listed and you rate your interest in the tasks on a five-point scale. When you take these inventories you will project if you might like the task without worrying about talent or training (that's what college is for). It's best to stay out of the middle when answering these questions, as you won't come up with a strong preference for anything. I like the O*Net site (www.onetonline.net) because you can search for careers from the profiler questions after you finish the inventory. You can also see job outlooks for the future and levels of education needed to prepare for each job. You can spend all day on this site. There is just that much information! This is all great information, but it's also good to keep in mind that the job you accept after graduating from college might not even have been invented yet. Years ago, who would have thought that someone could get paid to be in charge of social media for a company and spend all day on Twitter and Instagram?

I use and like tools like the ones listed above, but my personal philosophy is that it's OK to go to college undecided. College is a great time to learn more about yourself as a person and develop new interests and skills. I also understand where parents are coming from when they think about how much money is spent on college and want to make sure that their kids will be a successful candidate in the job market upon graduation.

1. I want to learn about my personality type. Can you help?
2. I'm OK with being undecided, but my parents want me to declare a major. Can we talk about it?

Chapter Seven

Finding the Fit

This chapter deals with the work and reflection that goes into coming up with colleges that will potentially be an academic, social, and financial fit for you and your family. At this point in my practice I ask parents to answer a few questions. These are not easy questions and require some deep thought about their child. They are, however, very important. A student may be interested in attending a large university many states away that has a decent party scene and good academics. Insight from parents might indicate that this particular student might not be successful in very large introductory classes. This information is very helpful when thinking about where the student will be most successful as a college student. Introductory classes need to be passed so that the student can continue to enjoy the beautiful weather and fun atmosphere of SEC schools like the University of Florida, Georgia and others. Parents can do this part together or separately. In the case of divorce I will often get two sets of answers. This is great information for me.

Questions For Parents

1. Please comment on your child's strengths and weaknesses as a student. Please comment on your perspective on your

student's motivation, self-discipline, energy level, organization, independence, creativity, level of confidence, etc.
2. How would you describe your child's personality and values? Please comment on leadership, maturity, concern for others, social and/or community interests, etc.
3. Please comment on your child's growth and development in the last three years.
4. What is your child's greatest accomplishment to date? How does your child stand out from the crowd? Any special characteristics or abilities?
5. Please indicate any family, medical, psychological or special testing background so that I can effectively counsel you during the college selection process. Are there any adversities that your child has had to overcome, which have been instrumental in his/her current level of competency? Does your child have an IEP or 504 plan? If so, please elaborate.
6. What characteristics are you looking for in a college/university for your child? You might comment on type of school, size, academic programming, location, sports, etc.
7. Please list colleges/universities to which you will encourage your child to apply.
8. Please list five words to describe your child.
9. Is there anything else that you would like to add?

The form that I send to parents electronically gives plenty of space for the answers and I expect thoughtful responses. Parents are often experts on their children, afterall.

One of the things that takes so much time during the college process is doing research. You may need to research different majors or figure out what the difference is between civil engineering and civil technology. You may really, really, really love college hockey....to watch. It would make sense to do some research to see which schools have decent hockey teams. There are so many things that you can (and should) research when it comes to colleges. I've devised a quick questionnaire that I have students' fill out. It's not a definitive list of priorities, but rather an exercise in thinking about what might work for you.

Geographic location

Please rank in order of importance:

Northeast____

Mid-Atlantic____

South____

Midwest____

Mountains/Southwest____

West Coast_____

Doesn't matter_____

Setting

Urban_____Suburban_____Rural_____Doesn't matter_____

Size (total students)

Very small (under 1,500 students)____

Small (1,500-3,000)____

Medium (3,500-6,000)____

Large (6,000-15,000)____

Very large (15,000+)____

Doesn't matter_____

Type of institution

College (mostly undergraduate students)_____

University (under grad and graduate students)_____

Doesn't matter_____

Coeducational_____

Single sex_____

Doesn't matter_____

Religious affiliation_____

Doesn't matter_____

Atmosphere

Conservative____

Traditional_____

Middle-of-the-road_____

Liberal_____

Doesn't matter____

What aspects of a school are 'must have'? ex: good ice hockey team

What characteristics would you like to avoid?

Intended major (if known)_____

Possible majors (if undecided)_____

Academic interests aside from major:

Which colleges are you interested in at this point and why?

Have you visited any colleges?

Which ones?

Best part of each school?

After you've thought about these questions you are ready to go onto one of the many search engines that will walk you through different choices and options. I typically use the BigFuture college search site on the CollegeBoard website (www.bigfuture.collegeboard.org) as I mentioned earlier. If you create a free account, then any searches you do can be saved. Also, you may already have an account if you've taken the PSAT or SAT. The BigFuture search has a lot of boxes to check and you certainly don't have to answer every question. If you answer the ones that are important to you it will produce a better result.

I also use these answers to think about schools that I've seen which might be a good fit for the student. I am always happy to make suggestions and will do my own research based on the results of this questionnaire as well as the parent questionnaire and conversations with the student and parents. This is when I will present you and your parents with a college list as a place to begin your search.

There are ten tabs on the left hand side of the page of the BigFuture site. Try to be specific on stuff that matters. If you are too general you might get hundreds of matches. It's also possible to get zero matches based on answers. If either happens you can go back and change a few things. Once you do this a few times you will get the hang of it. I've described some of the options below:

- **Test scores/selectivity.** If you have test scores you can add them in here. It's a good way to make sure that you are in the ballpark for a good academic fit. Having said that, there are more and more test-optional schools every year and some are quite selective. Some of them may ask for something in lieu of scores (more research!). The selectivity refers to the percentage of people who apply that are accepted. The higher the selectivity the lower the percentage of people accepted (think Ivies). If you don't have test scores, but have a pretty good feeling of where you will end up with selectivity you can just choose the box that corresponds to your feeling. This would be something

like the school accepts less than 25% (most selective) or accepts more than 75% (less selective).
- **Type.** This refers to things like size and other factors.
- **Location.** You can put in a region or a state or even a region and a state like New England plus New York
- **Campus and Housing.** This is where you can put in a preference for special housing or if you are interested in housing guaranteed for all four years (this seems to be more important in cities).
- **Majors and Learning Environment.** Here is where you can indicate a preference for schools with study abroad programs-yup, most of them have them. You can also add your major to make sure that only schools that have your major will show as a match. If you are undecided that is fine.
- **Sports and Activities.** Here you can check a preference for ice hockey and opera, if those are of interest. It is also where you can indicate a preference if you'd like to play sports in college. You will be asked to indicate gender, sport and division.
- **Academic Credit.** If you have a lot of high AP scores and wonder which schools will give you credit you can indicate that here.
- **Paying.** Here you can indicate how much you'd like to pay for college, which I don't pay much attention to, but you can also see which schools meet full financial aid and which ones have work-study programs.
- **Support Services.** Either academic or mental health.
- **Diversity.** If diversity is important this will match you with schools with a certain percentage of minorities or highlight just the Historically Black Colleges if that is of interest.

At any point you can close the question box by clicking on the X in the top right corner and see all the matches. Once you see the matches based on your answers you can see the CollegeBoard write up on the school and/or link directly to the college website.

1. I didn't see any colleges that I like on BigFuture. Can you recommend another search engine that might be better?
2. Can you give me three schools to visit so that I might get an idea of what I like?

Chapter Eight

Demonstrated Interest

What is demonstrated interest and why should you care? Both are good questions. Many colleges have a system to track your interest in them. This could be the result of the Commonapp. Colleges were starting to see what they called stealth applications after the introduction of the Commonapp, which makes it easier to apply to several schools. These applications were from students who had, prior to the submission of their application, shown no interest in the school.

These stealth applications proved problematic for colleges because colleges really only want to admit students who will at least consider attending. Many colleges are very careful to track their numbers and if a large number of students who are accepted decide to attend then this is very, very good for the school. A very qualified student who applies, but hasn't demonstrated any interest is a bit of a risk for colleges because they have no idea how interested (probably not very if he hasn't even signed up for mailings) this student is and how likely he is to attend if accepted. If he is that great a candidate for their school then he is also a great candidate for other schools. Colleges don't want to mess up their numbers!

Demonstrating interest is easy and can be done in several ways. In some cases it might even tip the scales in your favor. If you are vying for a spot and are as equally qualified as a student who hasn't demonstrated any interest then the spot may go to you!

Visiting

Visiting is the first and obvious choice for demonstrating interest. Make sure to register in advance and sign in when you get to admissions. Sometimes you will get a business card from your student tour guide at the end of the tour. If you have questions for them feel free to contact them. That is another touch point and sign of demonstrated interest. Please don't contact them just to demonstrate interest-everyone is busy!

Social Media

Social media is an easy way to demonstrate interest. 'Like' the school on Facebook, follow them on Twitter, Instagram and even Pinterest. If the school is in snow country you will see lots of pretty pics of the first snowfall. Also, if you are into sports do the same with the sports team that you are interested in. If you hate basketball, but love women's hockey then follow the women's hockey team and skip men's basketball unless you want to see promotional posts before every game. In other words, just follow what you are interested in.

Mailing List

You can also get on a mailing list by going online and telling the college a bit about yourself. This will be mostly demographic information and maybe something about what you'd like to study. You will get mail – email, regular mail and probably both. Some schools have virtual tours on their websites where you can actually demonstrate your interest as you tour the college from your bedroom. You will need to register for the virtual tour and this will put you on a marketing list so make sure it's a school that you won't mind hearing from.

Email to Admissions

Even emails to admissions to ask a quick question are often documented, but don't overdo it here. Emails to professors could count as well. Almost all emails to colleges should come from students and not parents.

College Fairs

If you are at a college fair and fill out the info card, you will be put on a mailing list and this will show interest. Be careful how many ways you contact the school to get on their mailing lists and make sure that you use the same name every time. I have gotten duplicate mailings from colleges under both Ellie Duley and Eleanor Duley and it's really frustrating. Especially if you care about the health of the planet!

Email Representative

If you take a business card from the admissions rep at a college fair and email her later this is also a form of demonstrated interest. If you have a burning question for the rep and don't hear back immediately it may because she is on the road doing other fairs so be patient.

Meet With Rep at High School

You may have a chance to learn more about a school and demonstrate interest when college reps come to your school. You will most likely sign up in guidance. You may even have a chance to talk with the rep one-on-one if other students can't make it to the meeting. Admissions representatives will get a list of students who attend the meeting and will use that to generate an email contact list. It will demonstrate your interest.

No matter how you demonstrate interest you will most likely end up on a marketing or mailing list. This is one reason to be careful and deliberate about where you demonstrate your interest. You could get mailings and emails from colleges for years so don't just contact a bunch of schools that you aren't really interested in and ask for more info. On the other hand, if you even think you might be interested go on and demonstrate some interest. Colleges love to feel the love.

When it's time to apply and you haven't visited or demonstrated interest in any way you should email admissions to express your interest. This is a last ditch effort type of thing and it's better to demonstrate the interest early in the college search process. I have students do this if they add a college to their list in the fall of senior year and can't make it to the school for a visit.

Lastly, there are schools that don't track demonstrated interest, but I like to think that it's better safe than sorry.

1. What schools don't track demonstrated interest?
2. Can I demonstrate interest without getting all that mail?

Chapter Nine

Road Trip

We've already covered that sophomore year is a good time to get on some campuses to get an idea of what is appealing in a college. You will be spending four years somewhere so it makes sense to figure out what suits. Junior year is time to get serious about those visits. This is when you will pull together all the research that you've done on colleges and go on a college visit road trip to visit schools where you think you might like to apply. Hopefully, mom and dad will help you with the travel arrangements.

Some colleges really track your demonstrated interest (or how often you've had contact with the college) and the best way to demonstrate interest is to visit. Make sure that you sign up for an info session and tour, most schools have this info online, and don't forget to sign in when you get to admissions. If any of your schools require an evaluative interview or offer a non-evaluative interview you should see if you could do this while you are on campus. I always suggest that students take advantage of non-evaluative interviews as this is a chance to have any questions answered and have a conversation with someone in admissions about what it would really be like to attend that school.

Dressing for college tours is mostly common sense. If your high school has a dress code, you certainly wouldn't want to bust out any items that would be problematic at school. Wear comfortable clothes and shoes and pay attention to grooming. If you are interviewing, you might want to step it up a bit.

I tour about 30 schools a year. Sometimes I go with a counselor tour so there are only counselors in the group. These are great because other counselors will often come up with interesting questions. Other times I will tag along with families. These are really interesting because usually only the parents ask questions and they are questions that parents care more about. On one tour the mom was absolutely fixated on seeing what the dorm bed would look like on risers, which are something that you can buy and bring to school. They raise the bed about eight to 12 inches and make for more storage under the bed. They also were apparently too high for her daughter....just don't use them in this case. This conversation took up about ten minutes of the tour-I kid you not! It's not a bad idea to split up if there are two or more tour guides going out at the same time. You can compare notes afterwards and students can ask questions that are important to them without their parents dominating the conversation. I like to think of it as divide and conquer as long as you share notes and thoughts later.

Pictures

One thing that I always do when I first get to a college campus is take a picture of the name of the college—either on the main sign, a flag or a building-once I took a picture of a maintenance vehicle because the name of the school was on the door. I do this to identify that the pictures that follow will all be from this institution. This is especially helpful if you tour more than one school in a day or if you're touring several schools over the course of a few days. I try to take a lot of different pictures of things that interest me and will remind me of the campus when I look at them later. I try not to take a bunch of classroom pictures-usually one will do.

There are schools that request that you don't take any pictures, like MIT for example, and you must be respectful of this. There also may be places within the school where they don't want you to use a flash-again, please respect their wishes. This allows your tour guide to do her job without getting distracted and reprimanding her guests. It's also embarrassing if you get singled out.

Tour Guides

A note about tour guides. They are more often than not students of the college. A lot of them are paid, but some are volunteers. They are, literally, just a few years older than you are. They tell the same lame jokes over and over and their spiel is often the same. Some schools will give tour guides a general script and others give them the ability to personalize the tour based on the group. Give them a break if they seem to be having an off day. They might be worried about a class or maybe a broken relationship. As much as you shouldn't pick a college based on wanting to be friends with a really great tour guide, you should try not to let a less than stellar tour guide affect your perception of the school. Also, try not to let lousy weather ruin your perception of a school as every state has a rainy season.

It appears that I did the opposite: Many years ago I toured the University of Maine in early October. The leaves were beautiful, the sky was a perfect chamber of commerce blue, blue bear paws (the mascot is a Maine black bear) were painted on the sidewalks and the vibe was amazing. I was sold! In my case everything worked out spectacularly, but it's not the best way to pick a college. In my defense, I had toured other schools and done my research. The happy vibe was just icing on the cake for me.

Explore On Your Own

When the tour and info session are over, and if you have time, you should try to explore campus on your own-either literally on your own or with your family, but without a campus representative. Sometimes you can get vouchers for the dining halls in admissions. If not, most dining halls will take cash, but it's safe to ask first. I was on a cash-less campus the day before I was scheduled to tour and went to the Subway in the student union. I had a credit card with me, but not much else since I had walked over from my hotel. I jumped in line and ordered my turkey sandwich. When I got to the register I learned that they only accept student cards-no credit cards and no cash. I was super embarrassed as I explained why I was on a gated campus with very little information on how things worked. The women at Subway were very nice and suggested that I see someone about a voucher, but then a student came up and swiped his card to buy me lunch. It was a lovely gesture and I'll always remember it that way and not think that he may just have been in a hurry and wanted to get the clueless lady out of the way.

Talk With Students

Often you can get a coupon for a discount at the bookstore. While you are out and about see if you can talk with students to see how they like the school. I remember an especially gregarious tour guide who told a story of how her father walked around campus after her college tours. He would ask random students three quick questions: Do you love it? Hate it? Or ehh? The tour guide, who was a high school student at the time, was mortified, but she did get good information that most students loved their school. It's an unofficial survey, for sure, but other conversations came from these interactions. I've found that students are almost always happy to talk about their colleges.

Earlier this winter, I was walking through a local university in the snow with my 115 pound black Newfoundland dog who had a big red bow tied around his neck. Several students wanted to stop just to have some fur therapy, which makes his gigantic head swell to ridiculous proportions. While we were out and about, and meeting and greeting, we came upon a group who were putting stakes in the frozen ground in the middle of a formerly green and now white space. I asked what was going on and I probably won't get this correct, but it was an interdisciplinary project between an art class and a philosophy class, I believe. It was a structure for a vigil later that night. Even though it was cold and snowing the students were happy to tell me about this project. How cool is that?

I also look at how many students are representing their school by wearing sweatshirts and other gear. I was touring Clark in Worcester, MA and asked the tour guide if a lot of students took advantage of the Higher Education Consortium of Central Massachusetts by taking classes at any of the other (11 total) area colleges. He replied that he hadn't personally, and didn't know too many 'Clarkies' that did, but he often saw Worcester Polytechnic Institute (WPI) students on campus and he could tell this because they were always repping their school with WPI gear. I toured WPI the next morning and confirmed that a lot of students showed their school pride with lots of WPI stuff. The bookstore must make a killing!

The more schools that you tour the more anecdotes you will acquire, but for the purpose of getting started with college tours, I've provided some questions to ask and observations to look for to get you started on the following form.

College Visit Evaluation Form
College:

Date: **Time:**

(This could be important later when you are comparing colleges)

List one interesting academic fact:

List one interesting non-academic fact or tradition:

List two extra-curriculars:

Your impressions of the buildings (student union, dorms, library, etc. Are they in good shape or do things look run down?):

Safety (location of blue lights, safety info mentioned in tour/info session, proximity to town and community members on campus, general feel):

First impression of the students:

Do students have any trouble getting the classes that they need?

Do your GPA/SAT scores match up with this school?

What is the academic feel? Is it more competitive or collaborative? Can you see yourself attending classes here?

Any other observations about the school?

Any concerns about the school? (Is there anything that you must have in a school that is missing?)

Do you feel a certain vibe? Is it a good vibe?

Overall impression of the school:

Other questions that you can ask your tour guide are things like:
- Are cars allowed for freshmen?
- What is the policy in the dorms for overnight visitors?
- How's the food? Usually they will tell you the truth.
- Ask whatever you think will be important in your decision should you apply and be accepted.

Since you are looking for a good academic, social and financial fit in all the schools that will eventually be on your college list, you should take a look at the Net Price Calculator, (NPC) that is on every college's website. It is usually found in the financial aid section. A note of caution here-some are better than others and the more accurate the information that you put in the more accurate the result will be. It's a great idea to look at the NPC (or ask your parents to) before going to visit because you can drop in to the financial aid office if you have any questions.

1. Can I ask my tour guide about the social life at the school?
2. Can I ask my tour guide if she receives financial aid and if it's any good?

Chapter Ten

The List

When thinking about applying to college you will consider many different factors. You may want to be away from home and not quite close enough for parental drop-ins. This happened to someone I know years ago. His parents traveled two hours early on a weekend morning. It happened to be when he was living in a fraternity house and it also happened to be the morning after a party and the cleanup process had not yet begun. He was called to the front door, spoke with his parents for a minute, they left and it was never mentioned again. Yikes.

The thing with being a few hours away or less is that it makes getting home pretty easy. Whether for holidays, breaks or just to do laundry and eat some of moms best cooking you will eventually come home from college for a visit. It's also really nice for parents to be able to drop you off at school and return home in one day. Some people can drive five hours and turn right around and do it again for the return trip. My son went four and a half hours away and that first year was tough. By sophomore year we happily paid for parking, gave him a used car and let him do the driving. I'm pretty sure that this was our idea...

Back in the day, it was about a 14-hour drive or a couple of flights away for me to go home from college. I found people to take me in for Thanksgiving and fall break because there just wasn't enough time to drive and it was too expensive to fly for three or four days. Are you the type of person who can go all semester without seeing family or pets?

Definitely don't discount how much you will miss Fido and Fluffy. I see students' everyday at the university in my town and if I'm walking my dog the students are not shy and come over for a visit. They always tell me what kind of dog they have and how much they miss him. This has, literally, happened on the third day of school! It's usually freshmen that are missing their dogs, but I've also taken him to rugby and soccer games and he is quite popular with all ages. This is definitely something to think about if you are looking at schools that are pretty far away. If your dog sleeps in your bed every night you will definitely miss that-even if you are only an hour away, but if you are close at least you can get home to visit Fido occasionally.

So, location is definitely a factor to consider. You also want to make sure that every school on your list meets your basic needs and that you feel that you will be happy there. If you can't say that about a school then why apply? You will most likely have three different levels of schools on your college list; some, you will be very sure that you have a good shot to get into (some call these safety schools), the next level are schools that you are likely to get into and you will probably have some schools that are a reach for you, but worth a shot. What you need to avoid is applying to schools just because you'd like to have that bumper sticker on your car (or you mom would like it).

Let's talk a little about safety schools. I like for everyone to have an academic and a financial safety school. Sometimes these are actually the same school and often it ends up being an in-state school. Be careful, though, if you aren't excited and willing to go there then it really isn't a safety school-it becomes a school where someone made you apply. If money isn't a factor then don't worry about having a financial safety school, but it's always a good idea to have an academic safety.

Likely schools are a little tricky. These are the schools where everything lines up and looks great on paper. That doesn't mean that you will automatically be admitted. What looks great on paper, (scores align, GPA is right in their median range and you wrote a fantastic essay), is never a sure thing. I worked with a young man several years ago who applied to mostly small liberal arts colleges in the mid-Atlantic region. He was perfect on paper. He was denied at most and wait-listed at one. He also had applied to an out-of-state state school, where he was granted admission. He was devastated with all the denials and considered taking a Gap year and reapplying because you just never know from year to year what colleges will get for applicants. He also considered trying to wait to see about the waitlist school. I called the college for him and was told that eight students had been taken off the list the prior year. He, ultimately, decided against both plans and, after a visit, attended the out-of-state flagship and loved his experience. College is really what you make of it!

I had another student in the same situation, but he did take the Gap year. He traveled across the country on his own and did research on colleges while honing his photography skills. He applied, and was accepted to, schools in a far-away region and was very happy with his choice. Was he accepted due to a geographical advantage? Who knows, but it worked for him. He matured a lot over that year and his application was a lot stronger for his experience. I didn't have a lot of influence over the lists of either of these young men, but it probably wouldn't have mattered since they thought they knew just what they wanted at the time and they both looked good on paper. The lesson here is that likelies are not givens and many of the selective schools are getting more and more qualified applicants every year. I think the sting of a rejection from a likely is much harder to take than the rejection from a school that is more selective. If this happens to you, you should take a little time to feel badly and then move right on with planning your future.

Reach schools, or schools that are a bit above your profile, (the combination of test scores, GPA, rigor etc.), are fun to think about, but you need to be realistic about your chances of admission. Don't get too down on yourself if you don't get into a school that accepts six percent of all applicants from all over the world. That's a big pot of competition right there. Something else about reach schools that you should think about is how good is the academic fit? If you do get in, will you be way over your head academically? Will everyone else have had the opportunity to take more advanced classes in high school and be way ahead of you in the classroom? It happens and is definitely something to think about. Another thing to think about is whether you will find peers at this fabulous school. A small liberal arts school that has a large number of students who aren't on financial aid may be a tough spot for someone who needs a lot of aid and can't participate in expensive road trips and sunny spring breaks. Some people are fine with this situation, but it's something that you may want to consider if you think that you would feel left out. This is where social fit is important. College is a lot of work, but it can be a lot of fun, too. Another note on social fit-if you can't wait to join and become president of the college Democrat club you may not be happy at an ultra conservative school and vice versa. If you don't care at all about politics this may not be a factor, but you should make sure that the schools to which you apply will satisfy all the things that you are really passionate about.

Now that we've identified the types of schools that you should consider the big question is to how many schools should you apply? I get asked this all the time. I appreciate that students want to have choices and an opportunity to compare a lot of financial aid packages, but applying to 20 or more (!) schools really just delays your final decision until April. If you do this and get accepted at ten schools you will now have to make a decision between ten schools. You will probably want to visit them all again and this makes for a very busy spring! By whittling your list down in the fall and targeting schools that you'd really want to attend you will reduce the number that accept you. Having a choice between five schools and ten is huge when you are trying to visit each during the month of April. Some people say fall in 'like' with a lot of schools and don't just fall in 'love' with one. I agree, but think applying to 20 schools is over the top. It's also very expensive because application fees run from free, up to $75 or more. Getting acceptances is fun and super exciting, but I've seen kids lose sleep over their final decision when they have too many choices!

So, back to the question of how many schools. The Common Application (www.commonapp.org) makes it easy to apply to many schools with just one application. In fact, you can apply to 20 just on the Commonapp and there are other application platforms out there. I like to see lists of between eight and ten schools. I really think that is plenty. Also, the FAFSA only lets you list ten schools at one time. There are ways around this, but really, ten is probably enough!

Your list will probably be pretty fluid. You will visit schools that you thought sounded great and take them off your list and you might add schools as you get closer to application deadlines, (more about these later). This is perfectly fine. When I was much younger I decided, quite definitively, that I would go to college in Boston. I applied to exactly zero schools in Boston when all was said and done. Seventeen-year-olds change their minds. A lot.

As important as the list is, balance in the list is equally important. You should have at least one safety, (as I mentioned, you should have one for academic and one for financial unless they are the same school or finances aren't of concern). I would shoot for three to five likely schools and one or two reach schools. All of these schools should be schools that you will be excited to attend. As you apply you may be more excited about some schools over others, but in the end you need to feel that you will be comfortable at all of your schools.

1. Can you help me come up with a college list?
2. Is three reach schools too many?

Chapter Eleven

Letters of Recommendation

Colleges seem to be all over the place with letters of recommendation. While some don't want to see any, others like to see two from teachers. Most want a letter from a school counselor, but some realize that some states have really high counselor case loads, I'm looking at you, California, and don't require a counselor letter. There are some schools that are very specific with what they are looking for, this is about you, MIT. I'm going to go through the basics of letters of rec., but you should do your research for each school to make sure that you are giving them what they want. It's also important not to offer too many letters-especially if they could potentially say basically the same thing about you.

Counselor Letter of Recommendation:

This is the standard and sometimes minimum requirement for colleges. It is a letter that looks at the whole student and, if written well, tells the college a bit about how the student fits into the high school community. I always tell my private clients to get to know their counselor because as a former school counselor who wrote many letters of recommendation for seniors, I can tell you, absolutely, that it's much easier to write about a student who you know.... And preferably, know well.

The counselor letter should only tell the college things that can't be found in the application. There is no need to list what class rank the student has because counselors also have to fill out part of the application, which covers things like class rank, GPA and disciplinary history. You will probably never see your counselor letter of rec. The only reason you might see it is if you ask for a copy to apply for scholarships later, but it will, almost certainly, be after the letter has been sent to colleges and safely tucked in your file. The take-away here is to give your counselor something great to write about by getting to know her.

You will most likely have a senior meeting with your counselor where you will discuss post-secondary plans. If you plan to go to college you may discuss a college list. You will probably also talk about other things so that the counselor can get to know you, if she doesn't already. I used a list of questions similar to the ones that I ask my clients to fill out. Counselor letters are supposed to be honest so not all counselor letters are stellar. I'm only including this because I want you to know that it isn't your counselor's job to sell you to your colleges.

Along with the letter, the counselor is often asked to rank the student in certain categories such as academic and school involvement. Counselors can also ask the college to have a phone conversation regarding the student. This would be if there was something that counselor didn't want to put in writing, but needed to be explained or addressed. I didn't have to do this with many students when I was a school counselor, but sometimes it is necessary and not really anything that student would know about unless the counselor disclosed this.

A note about the disciplinary question that is on most college applications. This is a little tricky because the student has to answer if they have seen disciplinary action during high school and the counselor does as well. You need to be on the same page on this.

It's better to own up to something, (especially if it happened freshman year), and show that you've learned and grown from the experience than to pretend it didn't happen. I had a student and his family spend an entire weekend stressed out because he asked a school employee, (not a school counselor), if he needed to answer the question affirmatively. The advice was wrong. The infraction was small and happened during his freshman year, but as a counselor I had to report it. Now we had his part of the application saying that he hadn't been in trouble and mine saying that he had. It could be argued that it could look like he was lying though that was not his intention. It was resolved by him writing a letter to the schools to which he had already applied. It was a very small infraction with a punishment that might have been too stiff for the crime and all ended up fine, but talk about adding stress to an already stressful time... A quick conversation about his intention would have saved us all a lot of stress and worry!

I also saw another counselor deal with a phone call from a school because the student owned up to her infraction, but didn't go into the delicate details. This call was initiated by the college. Stuff happens; you just need to be prepared to deal with it.

Teacher Letters of Recommendation:

These letters generally speak to the academic performance of the student and the best teacher letters give an example or anecdote. Students with close to perfect academic records might get similar letters from different teachers so this is why I like the addition of an anecdote. You probably won't see your teacher letters, either.

You will want to check the school requirements for teacher letters. MIT, for example, would like to see a letter from a math or science teacher and another letter from a teacher in Humanities. Most college admissions representatives agree letters should be from teachers that the student had junior or senior year. The information from a freshman year teacher is just too old and so much growth has hopefully happened between 9th and 12th grade. If you have a teacher senior year that you also had freshman year then this might be a good choice and an opportunity to demonstrate that maturity.

I always tell students to ask the teacher if he is willing to write a letter on their behalf. With most of the application platforms, which will be discussed later, the student will invite the teacher on the application and the teacher will get an email with instructions on uploading the letter directly to the application and, in turn, the college.

I have had teachers come into my office to let me know that a student on my caseload put them as a reference without asking. They never came in to tell me this conversationally and were usually pretty mad at both the student and me. This is wrong and never ends well. I tell students to give the teacher their first deadline AND ask the teacher at least two weeks before this deadline.

In the different public schools where I've worked I've noticed that some teachers are heavily sought out for letters, which they generously write on their own time. Some teachers will ask for a resume or list of things that the student has done in high school to help them write the letter. Again, I prefer the teacher letter to be more about their experience with the student. If the teacher seems unsure about writing a letter for you then it might make sense to move on and ask another teacher.

Other types of Letters of Recommendation:

Employer letters are good for a student who has a lot of responsibility at work and wants the college to know about it. It's certainly not essential for every student who has a job to ask his boss for a letter, but if the student is working in the field in which he would ultimately like to pursue a degree, it might make sense.

Clergy letters of recommendation are important for a student who is very involved with his place of worship. Mormon students applying to colleges within their faith will most likely have to get these as part of the application, but if they are applying to a school outside of their faith then this letter can speak to the level of dedication within the church. I would only advise getting this type of letter if the student is very involved with his place of worship and if this is a large part of who he is as a person.

Outside activities letters of recommendation might be from an Eagle Scout leader if the student is getting his Eagle Scout rank. If a student volunteers teaching younger students dance for several hours a week, a letter here might make sense. It really depends on what else the student has going on and how strong the letter might be. It's definitely case-by-case.

So, how many letters is too many? I advise students that five letters is the very top. Anything more will probably be duplicative and just too much for admissions representatives to read. More is not better in this case. Most students will submit with a counselor letter and two teacher letters. This is definitely a part of the application that requires some thought before action.

Some schools give seniors 'brag sheets' to help counselors with their letters. They may also give you sheets to give to teachers. These are usually not for teachers who will be writing you a letter of rec. They sheets are returned to the counselor and are used by the counselor to pull quotes from when the counselor is writing your letter. Many students find this really confusing (and it is), but it's done for a good reason and helps give the college many sides of you as an applicant.

1. How do I know if someone will write a good letter for me?
2. Can my parents write a letter of rec for me?

Chapter Twelve

The (dreaded) Essay

The application essay, sometimes called a personal statement, is one of the most important parts of your application. This is because it's a chance for colleges to get to know you aside from your GPA, class rank, test scores and rigor. This is a personal essay that is usually between 250-650 words, written in first person and nothing like you've probably done in high school. You should be prepared to spend a lot of time on your essay-especially if you are applying to selective schools. Your essay is used by admissions people to get to know you better, but they will also consider the essay as a sample of how you present yourself in writing. In other words, grammar counts.

The best essays take time. I start working on essays with clients over the summer between junior and senior year. You will need to have at least a partial college list before the essay so that you can determine which prompts you should consider. The Commonapp hasn't changed essay questions in a few years, but when they do change them they usually release the prompts before summer break. Schools that have their own application will use different prompts. I was working with a student who applied to the University of Florida a few years ago. They had one prompt for every applicant. I can't imagine reading thousands upon thousands of essays on the good life! It's not unusual for me to send an essay back for revision eight or ten times so starting early is really important.

Earlier, I mentioned that I ask parents for some input on the college process with some thought provoking questions. During the essay process, I ask the student for the same. These questions are also helpful when thinking about which colleges are good matches.

- How do you assess yourself as a student? What do you consider your academic strengths and weaknesses? Do you think that your transcript and test scores accurately reflect your ability?
- Did you have any special circumstances during high school that may have affected your achievement? Please explain.
- If you could change one thing about high school, what would it be and why?
- Have you experienced any unusual life circumstance, which shaped you into who you are today? Please explain.
- Please list ten words to describe yourself.
- What is the one thing that you'd like your counselor to highlight in your letter of rec.?
- And most importantly, what do you want the college to know about you that can't be found on any other part of your application?

I follow this up with a conversation where I have another set of questions that I ask. These questions are taken from the senior interview that I developed when I was a public school counselor.

These questions foster conversation and help me to understand what is important to the student. I remember going through this interview with a top student (scores, GPA, activities, leadership—the whole package), when we got to the question about what he had learned about himself through his leadership experience he just put his head in his hands. He had never been asked a question like this and had never thought about his experiences in this way. He's a great kid and we talked through it. I'd like to think I taught him something about self-reflection that day.

There will be questions that don't really apply to every student and that is fine. There are also questions that will really stump a student. Depending on the question and the student I might spend some time probing to see if there is anything that might be helpful to know. I will often find obvious essay topics that the student might not think of without this exercise.

The dream job question is just for fun. I preface the question that they don't need to make a good living at this job and they don't need to have any talent. Most students will answer with a job that is related to what they'd like to study. I'm really looking for the kid who's hiding his inner rock star and occasionally, I've been rewarded with this answer. It's a good way to end a serious conversation with a laugh!

- Do you know what you plan to study?
- What schools are you thinking about? Why?
- Have you visited any? Which ones?
- Do you know what you are writing your college essay on and why?
- Volunteer work? Why did you choose it and what did you get from it?
- Leadership experience:
    - What type of leader are you?
    - What have you learned about yourself through leadership?
- How have you grown in HS and what changed most?
- What do you do in your spare time?
- Describe a non-academic achievement that you are proud of:
- Have you overcome adversity in your life? If so, how?
- Strengths/weaknesses:

- Has any one thing/person had an impact on your life? How?
- Tell me one thing about you that I won't find on your college application...
- Dream job:

After our interview session I have a pre-writing exercise that I use with students that combined with the other work they've done and the interview, may or may not, turn into a college essay. The brainstorming and pre-writing exercise is designed to be done quickly without regard for punctuation and grammar. As opposed to the questions and interview I really don't want clients to think about these questions too much. I try to do the pre-writing exercise about a week after the interview. I don't like to overwhelm students with too many questions in one sitting, and the better the answers are, the more the student will have to work with when it comes time to sit down and write the essay.

- If you really knew me, you would know...
- I'm happiest when...
- The best decision that I ever made was to....
- The worst decision that I ever made was to...
- The ten things that I could not (happily) live without...
- The five things that I want an admissions dean to know about me are:
- My favorite activity involves...
- I couldn't do what s/he asked because...
- It was the nicest thing anyone had ever said to me:
- My biggest failure is...

The landscape of college applications has changed dramatically in the last ten years and is continuing to change. Most of my students use the Commonapp, which gives the student seven prompts and asks the student to address one in an essay that is between 250-650 words. Here are the 2018-19 prompts:

1. Some students have a background, identity, interest, or talent that is so meaningful they believe their application would be incomplete without it. If this sounds like you, then please share your story.
2. The lessons we take from failure can be fundamental to later success. Recount an incident or time when you experienced failure. How did it affect you, and what did you learn from the experience?
3. Reflect on a time when you challenged a belief or idea. What prompted you to act? Would you make the same decision again?
4. Describe a problem you've solved or a problem you'd like to solve. It can be an intellectual challenge, a research query, an ethical dilemma – anything that is of personal importance, no matter the scale. Explain its significance to you and what steps you took or could be taken to identify a solution.
5. Discuss an accomplishment or event, formal or informal, that marked your transition from childhood to adulthood within your culture, community, or family.
6. Describe a topic, idea, or concept you find so engaging that it makes you lose all track of time. Why does it captivate you? What or who do you turn to when you want to learn more?
7. Share an essay on any topic of your choice. It can be one you've already written, one that responds to a different prompt, or one of your own design.

I have a worksheet that breaks each question down into keywords and helps structure the essay. According to the Commonapp, most (over 50%), of students answered question number 1 during the 2015 application season. This is a question that was phrased so that the student could virtually write about anything. We talk about all the questions before I ask which question jumps out as an obvious choice. I give examples of topics that I've seen for each question. I love question number two about failure, but I've only had a few students pick this one. I think kids are afraid to show that they've failed at something, but the most important part of that question is demonstrating that they have learned from the experience. Self-reflection and honesty are very important with this question. I also find that talking it out is very important with the failure question.

A few general thoughts before you begin…

- All of these questions require you to look within yourself.
- All answers should show growth and/or lessons learned.
- What makes you unique?
- What can you add to your application that the admissions people won't see anywhere else?
- Use description, but don't get caught up in all the little details. Take it to the next level and show critical thinking skills!

The following is taken from a blog post that I wrote in July of 2016, while some of it is repetitive, I believe that it's all good stuff.

So now that you've seen the Commonapp essay questions how about some tips?

Words. I have 2 things to say about words:
1. You have between 250-650 words. Plan on writing between 600-625 words-it's harder than you might think to be this concise and

> your essay will be chopped off at 650 words if you exceed the limit. Don't leave your readers, (aka admission officers), hanging by ignoring this detail. I advise going a bit short of 650-just in case.
> 2. Choose your words carefully. Not only is it hard to craft a memorable essay in 650 words or less-this means that every word counts-it's also important to choose words that aren't strange, scary or sound too much like you went to the Thesaurus. Believe it or not, many years ago I read an essay with the word nihilistic in it three times. I can't think of an essay that I want to read that has this word once, but three times? Like, what's your point, dude? And yes, I did have to look it up to make sure that I knew the definition because, frankly, it's not a word I use every day and it wasn't clear in context...any of the three times. I'm not making this up!

First person. I know that you don't write in first person in school, like, ever, but you need to figure it out for your college essay. That's all. You just need to figure it out.

Go deep. This tip is tied in with first person. You don't want to write a bunch of sentences like, I did this and I did that and aren't I great. You will need to do some reflection and examine what you did, why you did it, and what you learned from it. It all depends on your essay which of these questions that you will address, (preferably all three), and how you will address them. Just make sure to spend some time reflecting. This is a big part of what I do when I work with students. We spend a lot of time trying to draw the good stuff out. It's also better to go deep on one thing rather than trying to cover every detail in your 17 years.

A moment in time. This relates to going deep. A great college essay doesn't start with the day you were born or the day you started Kindergarten and declared that you would someday be a doctor. Sometimes a great essay can be just a moment in time. It's how you describe and relate to this moment that will make the essay memorable.

Set the scene. I'm really loving essays that start by setting the scene-just be careful to not spend too much time, (or too many words), leading up to what you really want your readers to take away from your essay.

At the end of the day the most important thing to think about when writing your essay is, "What do I want college admissions to know about me?" When I'm reading an essay and it seems to be getting off track I always go back and ask the student this question. Don't tell me about your cat unless you cat has something to do with what you want admissions representatives to know about you.

There are some topics that should be avoided if possible unless you have a really unique angle or reason for choosing that topic. I've heard many college admissions representatives say that they would be happy to never read another essay about winning the state championship or how a student tore his ACL and after months of rehab was back on the playing field the next season. A lot of students are passionate about sports, but I guarantee you that there is something else about you that will be interesting to your colleges. This is why I spend so much time asking questions and talking about other experiences.

Never be school specific in the Commonapp essay-it will go to all of your schools. Harvard doesn't want to know why you love New Haven! School specific essays are the supplemental ones described in the next chapter.

1. Can you help me brainstorm for my essay?
2. How many people should read my essay?
3. If I hate my essay should I try another prompt?

Chapter Thirteen

The "Why College X" Essay

The "Why College X" essay is the most common supplemental essay and it's mostly the more selective schools that ask for this extra piece of writing. These essays are usually around 250 words so your words really do matter here. Each and every one is important. In this essay, colleges are asking why you'd like to attend their particular school. It's a good time to show your knowledge of this school. This knowledge may be from a conversation or email exchange with a professor, from a visit or from research you've done on the website. You also want to let them know what you will bring to the party, so to speak. I had a conversation just last week with an admissions representative and we were talking about this question. I used the phrase, "What will you bring to the party?" and he quickly replied, "Not beer." We had a quick laugh, but colleges really do want to know what students will be bringing to their community—in the best sense possible.

Colleges are building a community with each and every class that they admit and want to admit students who will be engaged with that community. I think of the "Why College X" essay as a combination of what they have and how you will make use of it. You want to stay away from things that are too obvious, like the weather. Liberal arts schools in Florida know that they have warmer winters than the liberal arts schools in New England. Even if you are hoping to go there for the weather I'm sure that you can come up with something better for the essay! Below is a pretty typical question. Even though it says it's an optional question, it's my opinion that none of the optional questions are really optional if you want to present your very best application.

Students have many choices in their college search and application process. Please share why you have chosen to consider Stonehill among your possible college options. (Optional - 250 word maximum)

To tackle this question I might suggest that a student take a look at Stonehill's mission statement, which reads:

Stonehill College, a Catholic institution of higher learning founded by the Congregation of Holy Cross, is a community of scholarship and faith, anchored by a belief in the inherent dignity of each person.

Through its curriculum of liberal arts and sciences and pre-professional programs, Stonehill College provides an education of the highest caliber that fosters critical thinking, free inquiry and the interchange of ideas.

Stonehill College educates the whole person so that each Stonehill graduate thinks, acts, and leads with courage toward the creation of a more just and compassionate world.

There is a lot of good stuff in there. If a student is really into civil rights, writing something about that would make a nice and meaningful essay. If the student can't relate to anything in the mission statement then it's perfectly ok to go another way.

Some colleges will offer an optional essay that is often an opportunity to write in a bit of depth, (250 words), about an extracurricular activity. I really don't consider these to be optional and strongly suggest that students take advantage of this opportunity for the college to get to know them a little bit more. This is a place to describe your leadership style if you are an officer of a club or captain of a team. You can give an example, which gives the college more insight than the 150 characters allowed on the activities section of the Commonapp. You can also write about the hours that you spend babysitting your younger siblings so that your mom can pursue her dream of becoming a nurse. It's really an opportunity to explain something that you do in your spare time. It's a huge part of what makes you, you.

1. One of my questions is what's my favorite snack? How do I answer that?
2. Should I use humor in my why college X essay?

Chapter Fourteen

Activities (or what you do when you aren't in school)

Speaking of the activities section-this is a place to let colleges see what you do outside of the classroom. You can use this form to keep track of what you've done over your four years in high school. It's amazing how quickly we forget! If you have done more than this form allows then list them. You will have to prioritize them later.

School Activities. This is where you would list clubs.

1.

2.

3.

4.

School Sports.

1.

2.

3.

4.

Outside activities. This can include outside sports as well as things like dance, karate, community theater

1.

2.

3.

4.

Work/volunteer/summer activities.

1.

2.

3.

4.

Other hobbies and interests, especially if you spend a lot of time with them.

1.

2.

3.

4.

5.

This is a blog post from June of 2015 that explains why colleges care about what you do over the summer as well as in your spare time.

Junior year is almost over. Time to kick back and relax poolside, lakeside, beachside and hang out with friends 24/7, right? This sounds like the perfect reward for busting butt all year: acing classes and killing it on the SAT.

This sounds great, but it will get old and most importantly for the college going student, this is not what colleges want to see. It's also probably not

what parents want to see... and they're still probably paying for at least your cell phone. Got to keep them happy!

So, what is a rising senior to do? It's short and simple—get a job! You don't have to start your own business, (though you could), and babysitting does count. You don't have to have a big fancy summer plan or a trip to Europe to study classics to impress colleges.

Summer jobs provide students with money, (duh), but they are also great for other reasons.

Students who work in the summer might find themselves balancing many things like athletics, dance or music lessons, family vacations and the all-important social life. This sounds hard, but it's really great training for college where you will be pulled in many directions and it seems like you have endless amounts of time. Trust me, you won't have endless amounts of time. You may only be in class for 15 hours a week, but you will need to plan for many hours of study time each week as well. You will also be juggling clubs, sports, meeting new friends and other things that eat up a lot of time. Colleges like to see students with time management skills!

Summer jobs are also a great way to learn and practice leadership skills. You might work up to being a second key in a retail store or you may plan and execute a great outing for the kids you're babysitting. Leadership gained through a summer job could be a great college essay. Oh yeah, that's another thing you should be thinking about during free time over the summer.

Communication is key to having a summer job. Whether you are scooping ice cream and dealing with the sweet loving public or lifeguarding at the local pool, you will be dealing with all types of people (customers, bosses, parents-you get the picture). You will learn to advocate for yourself if you want to ask for time off or negotiate schedule changes with a co-worker. You will deal with upset people-you didn't really run out of triple chocolate brownie fudge???

You might even experience a bit of failure at your summer job. You might find out that you hate dealing with the public or that you can't pass a lifesaving course no matter how hard you try. This sounds awful, but it is still an opportunity. Essay, anyone? Showing how you dealt with, and what you learned from, failure can be a very powerful essay. Knowing what you don't like is just as important as knowing what you do. It's always better to experience failure before you go off to college and while you still have a great support system at home.

You will also learn about money management and perhaps budgeting. Colleges may not care as much about this unless you need that money to pay the bill! You will surely benefit from the experience when you go out to live on your own.

Sticking with a job all summer (even if you hate it) shows colleges that you can see something through. It also shows a certain level of maturity and colleges like this.

Basically, what it comes down to, is that colleges like students who have a bit of life experience. And yes, you can get this right in your own hometown.

There are certainly students who don't work during the summer because they are doing other things and this is OK. It's the, 'doing other things', part that is important. If you can't show colleges that you are doing things outside of school, then they may just assume that you are working on your tan or playing video games. As I've mentioned already, colleges are basically a community. A good community has members that care about it and work hard to make it better. This is true in college so colleges are looking to admit students who will contribute to their community in some way. It could be by joining clubs, playing sports or becoming a resident assistant or another job that you will take on campus.

What if you worked a lot in high school? This could be because you needed to help out with the family finances or it could be because you bought and restored your very first car. Having a job in high school is a very worthy use of your time. As I mentioned in the blog, you will learn a lot from having a job. When you fill out the activities section of the Commonapp you may only have work experience, but this is ok. It may be something that you'd like to add to the additional information section of the Commonapp. This is a section where you can add an essay of up to 650 words to explain something that isn't obvious elsewhere on the application. Most students don't use this, but it's there for students who would benefit from more explanation on a certain topic.

The following is taken from another blog that I wrote. I can't stress enough that you should pay attention to your activities (whether you are using the Commonapp or another application platform).

Here is what the activities section looks like:

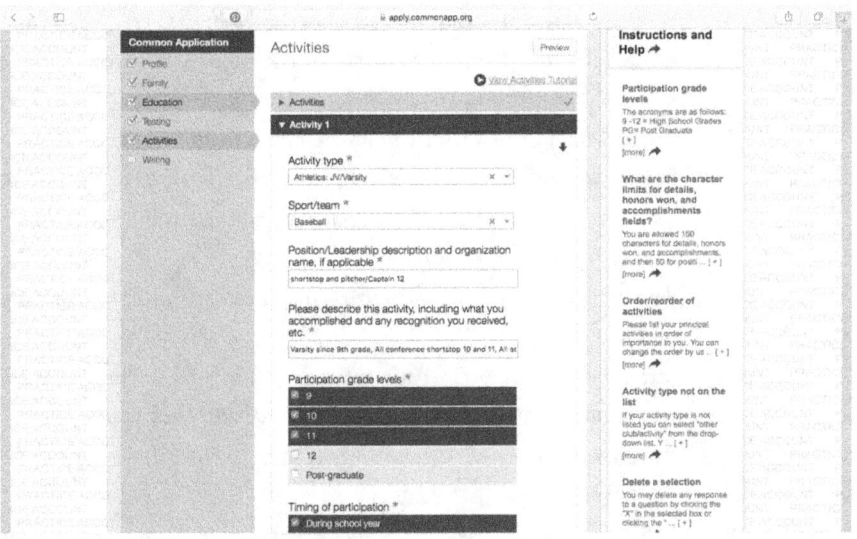

The activities section of the Commonapp might be more important than you think. Why do colleges care about your activities? It's simple, really. They want to know what you are up to when you aren't in the classroom. Why? Because colleges want students who will get involved in their college community. They also want to make sure that you aren't spending all your time goofing off!

So, back to the activities section of the Commonapp. There is room to list up to ten activities. Whether you have two activities or ten, you should prioritize them in order of importance to you. If you have more than ten that are really important then you might want to attach a resume, but that's another blog.

After you prioritize your activities you can fill out the section like this:

- There will be two drop down boxes-these are self-explanatory
- Position/Leadership line-this is limited to 50 characters. If your activity is a club then you will name the club. If you hold an office you will name that office. Get as much info into these 50 characters as possible.
- The next box asks you to describe the activity. Here you have 150 characters. Yes, I wrote characters and not words, but you need to write words so choose them carefully.
- Next is which grades that you participated in this activity. If it's in the summer that will be added to the year following that summer.
- Timing of participation is a dropdown and your choices are during the school year, break or all year.
- The next line is hours/week. If it's a sport count practice time and games.
- Next is weeks/year. Do your best here. Don't forget pre-season or any summer camps where you are involved with that activity.
- Do you intend to participate in this activity in college? It's OK if you don't!
- Lather, rinse, repeat and move on to the next activity. https://en.wikipedia.org/wiki/Lather,_rinse,_repeat

So what goes into the activities section? Here are some options:

Clubs

Sports

Drama

Band or youth orchestra-outside of school

Volunteering

Summer job

School year job

Babysitting younger siblings

Religious involvement other than just attending service

Hobbies

Foreign exchange travel

Some things to think about as you prioritize:

- *A sport that you played varsity in 9th grade and never continued probably isn't as important as one that you played for four years- even if you never started!*
- *Paid volunteer (one time) humanitarian trips are fine, but they really just show colleges that your parents can afford to send you. This alone does not show that you are passionate about saving the world!*
- *Not having a lot of activities because you either work to contribute to the family income or babysit younger sibs so parents can work is a very worthy use of your time.*
- *Working a part-time job so that you can have gas money and pay for car insurance shows maturity and money skills and there may be an opportunity to show leadership depending on the job.*
- *Did you start a dog walking business? There is so much good stuff here...*
- *Rebuilding an antique car? Think of all you've learned during this process.*
- *Helping elderly neighbors rake leaves every year? One time is probably not enough-especially if your parents made you do it.*
- *Do you write songs? Draw caricatures? Colleges want to know.*

The activities section is definitely a way to differentiate yourself from others so spend some quality time here.

1. I can't remember how many hours a week I spent in my freshman clubs. Can I just guess?
2. How important is being a captain?
3. I volunteered my freshman year and didn't continue. Does it count?

Chapter Fifteen

Application Platforms

I've been writing a lot about the Commonapp in this book because as I mentioned earlier, it is the application that most of my clients are using and it's a platform used by almost 700 colleges and universities. Not all schools use the Commonapp so be sure to check before opening an account.

The Common Application or Commonapp
(www.commonapp.org)

The Commonapp is just what it sounds like. It is an application that you fill out once and can use to send your application to up to 20 schools. It is free to create a Commonapp account though you will pay to send applications to schools. You will need to create the account with an email that you are ok with colleges seeing; dopedude@gmail is not OK. Also, make sure to write down your password as you will be in this application a lot! It takes about an hour to fill in the demographic info, but it's far better, in my opinion, to take the time here and not have to do it on a bunch of other applications. There is a common part of the Commonapp as well as school specific parts-remember the why college X essay chapter?

The common part includes information on you, (the applicant), as well as your family. The family part will ask if your parents attended college and if so where and when they graduated as well as their highest degree obtained. When I have my client's parents answer all the tough questions I also ask for all of this information so that it's readily available when it's time to fill out the application.

This is what the Commonapp tab looks like with my dog's demographic info. Notice the checkmarks in the left corner:

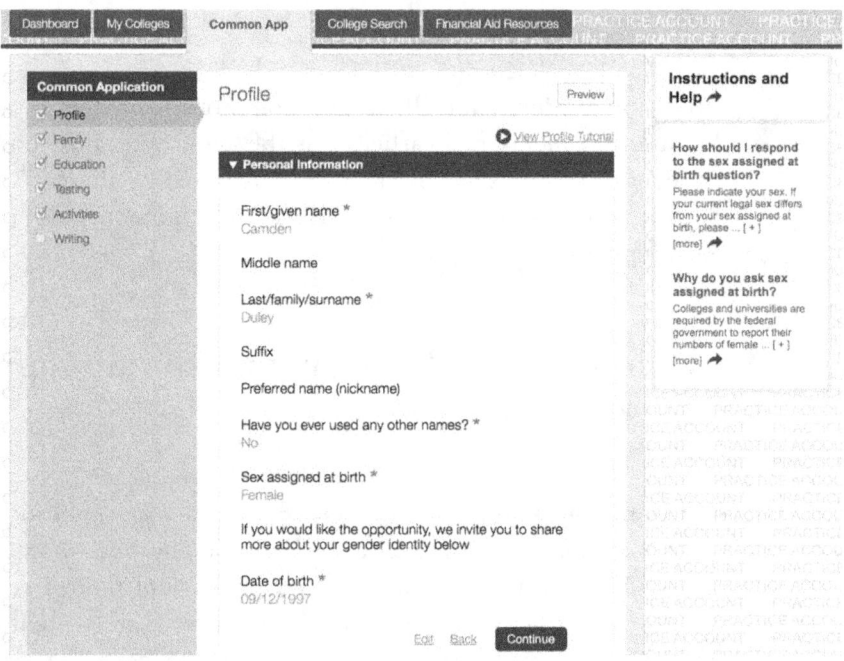

The common part also asks questions about testing. You can choose to self-report your test scores here if they will make your application stronger. The decision to do this or not is definitely case-by-case and depends on to which schools the applicant applies.

There is also a place for AP tests and scores. You should list the subject, but you probably don't want to self-report scores that are too low to give you credit at your schools.

The last two parts of the common area are the essay and the activities section as discussed in depth. The Commonapp is designed so that you can go in and out of it and add things as you find time and are ready. I find that my clients will do the demographics earlier and upload the essay last. When each section is complete you will be rewarded with a big green checkmark. This is a great visual to see if you've missed anything.

Once you have created a Commonapp account you can add colleges. There are five tabs across the top of the main page. You will use the Commonapp tab to fill out the six sections described above.

The dashboard tab will show a list of all the schools that you add. Once you've added schools you can go into the school specific questions and answer which decision plan you'd like, (early decision, early action, etc-these will be covered in the next chapter), you can use this section to keep track of deadlines. This tab is also where you will get the college specific questions and where you will assign recommenders. This is also where you will have an opportunity to share with the college if you intend to join certain activities and what you think you'd like to major in. Finally, this is where the supplemental essay questions will be if the college requires them. You will use the dashboard a lot in this process.

On the next page, you will see a screenshot of the Commonapp dashboard.

There is a tab to search for colleges, which is how you will add them to your dashboard. Colleges cannot see your dashboard so don't be afraid to add a college if you aren't 100% sure you will apply. This is NOT a way to show demonstrated interest. You can only have 20 colleges saved at one time, but deleting a college from your dashboard to add another that is more interesting to you is very easy.

On the next page, you will see a screenshot of the College Search page.

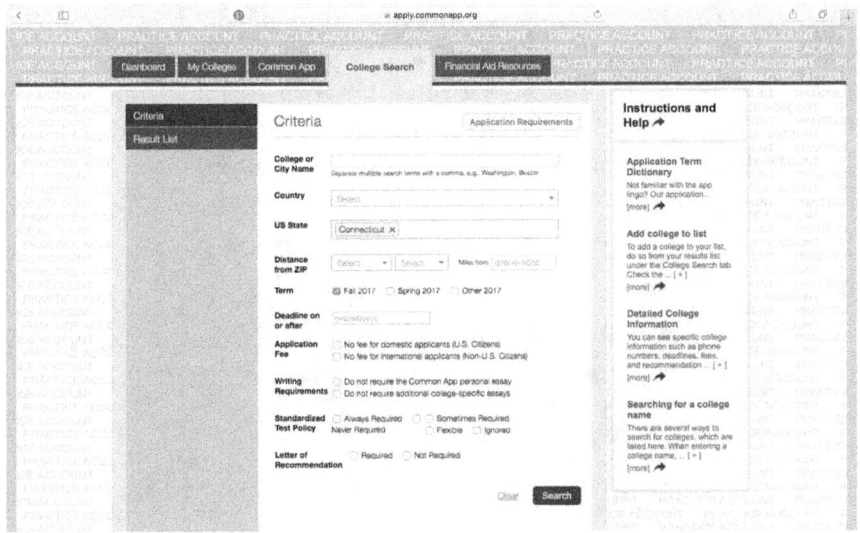

Here's a screenshot of college search results, below.

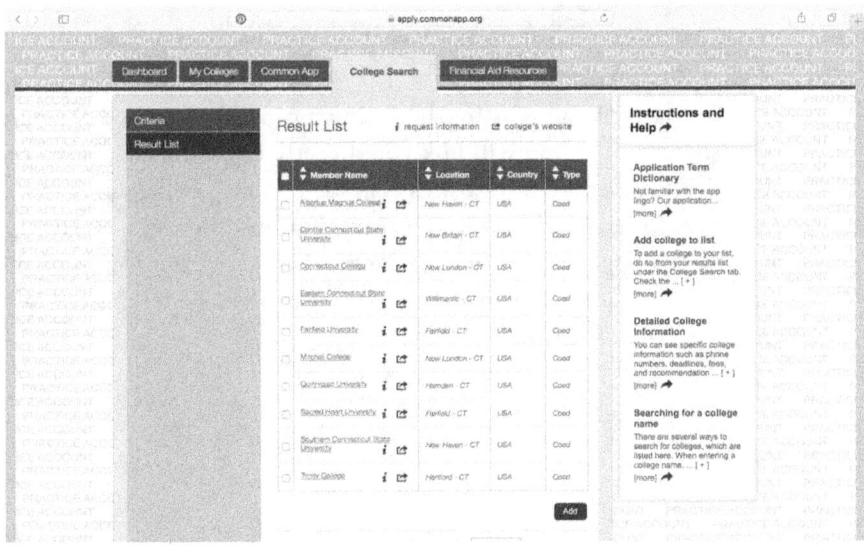

The My Colleges tab provides in depth information on the college deadlines and application requirements and can link you directly to the college website. On this example, you can see everything you would need to know about applying to Bates College. The fee is $60, they are test optional and the deadlines are clearly stated.

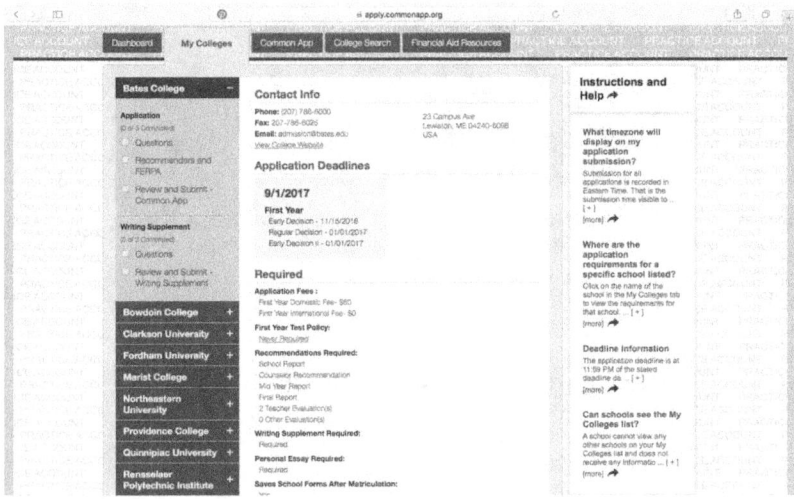

The last tab, shown on the following page, is named financial aid resources. This tab will link you directly to the financial aid page of individual college websites based on the colleges in your dashboard. Here you can find information on different scholarships that the college offers and, which, if any, require a separate application or essay. You can also get info on Federal loans and financial aid on the resource page.

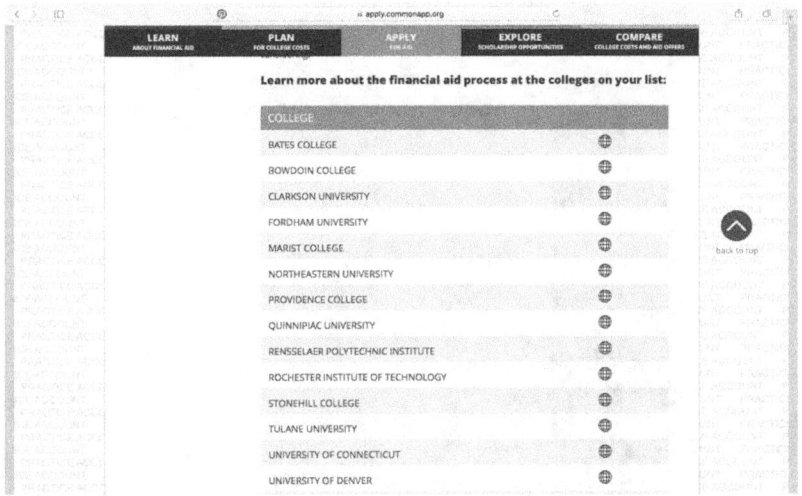

When you want to submit to a specific college you will access it from the dashboard and see what you still need to do before you are ready to submit. It should show that the Commonapp is done, (if it is), but may say that questions and recommenders are incomplete. The questions section will have four or five sections that all need to be completed. You will know that they are done when you see the green checkmark. **Often, the activities section will already have a green checkmark. This is because the answers are optional. Make sure that you open it to check for an optional essay that you really should write**.

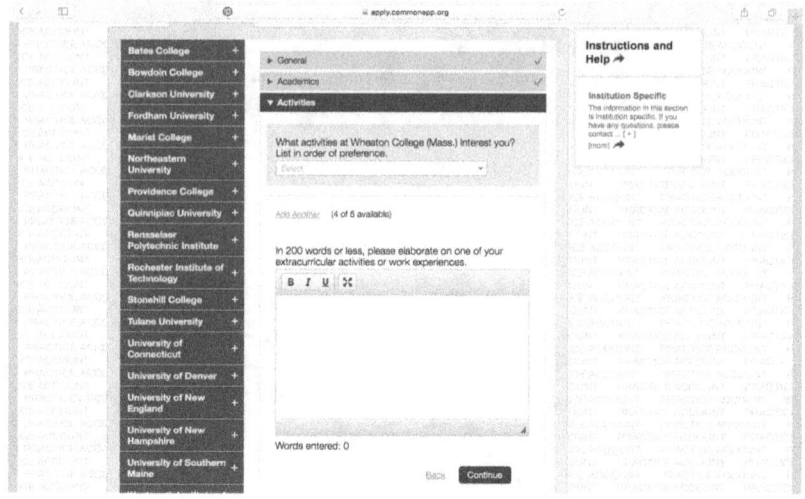

The FERPA, (Family Educational Rights and Privacy Act), and recommenders tab will ask you for a couple of things. You will read about FERPA and your right to see confidential letters of recommendation under certain circumstances. You will then be asked if you want to waive this right. You probably do. The reason you might waive this right is that it tells colleges that the letter hasn't been seen by you and that you had no influence over the contents. It makes the application more legit in the eyes of colleges. You will also have the opportunity to invite your recommenders here. Once they are entered into the system for one school you won't have to re-invite them, but you will have to manage them. If, for instance, you have a letter from clergy that you would like to go out to some, but not all, of your schools, you can do that here. By managing your recommenders, you can tailor who will submit to which schools. It sounds confusing, but will make more sense when you have your account open and can look at that page.

The last thing that you will do is review and submit. You will need to do this for each school. You want to make sure that your application looks exactly like you intend so that schools will see your very best application. This is your last chance to proofread before sending it off. Your essay may not be formatted just as you intended and I'm hoping that this will be fixed in the future. Colleges understand this glitch, but don't appreciate typos or bad grammar so proofreading is a must!

When you are ready, you will submit your application from the dashboard tab. You will be asked to electronically sign that all the work is your own and then you will pay the application fee. You will be notified that the application has been submitted. You will see this on your dashboard as well. You will also be able to see when the college downloads your application (usually two or three days later). You must apply to each school separately and you can do this over time. You should be very aware of any deadlines and be sure to submit prior to the deadline. With the Commonapp you have until midnight of the deadline date in your time zone to submit.

SlideRoom

SlideRoom is used by the Commonapp to offer students a way to submit a portfolio. Submission can be in videos, images or interactive media. The student will submit this after the Commonapp has been submitted to the school that the student wishes to add a portfolio and there is an additional charge for this service.

School Specific Applications

Many colleges and universities have their own application and you can apply right from their website. Some of these schools will also take other applications so it might not make sense to use their application if you are applying to a bunch of other schools that use one of the other platforms. Why fill out two if you can just fill out one application? The University of Maine system, for example, has a UMaine system application where you can apply to any or all of the four-year universities in the system. The application is a bit shorter than the Commonapp, but not as smooth when it comes to the release of records as students have to print this page out if it isn't available in the guidance office. The UMaine essay is aligned with the Commonapp and suggests 650 words maximum. It offers two prompts; topic of your choice and education and career goals. You only need to pick one so if you wrote an essay in English class for the Commonapp you can use it here as well.

Some schools will only use their application. I was researching the University of Pittsburgh for a client and realized that they only have an online application specific to their university. They have three short answer questions that aren't mandatory, but highly recommended that the student answer. These questions are expected to be a total length of 500 words. One question asks you to examine a time that you experienced failure, how you dealt with it and what you learned. The next question asks you to talk about your outstanding leadership and the third question is the why Pitt question. In 2015 the University of Pittsburgh received over 30,000 applications for 4000 admits. With this competition it seems that not answering these three questions would be a big mistake. The client that I was researching this school for ultimately decided not to apply. He had already filled out the Commonapp and written several essays. He also had not had a chance to visit and wasn't sure that he was that interested.

Massachusetts Institute of Technology (MIT) also has its own application. They also have a timeline of what they expect to happen when. For example, if you were thinking of applying to MIT in mid-December of your senior year then you have probably already missed the boat. MIT requires that all mandatory interviews be scheduled by early December. MIT requires five essays that range from 100 words to 250. There is a why MIT question, (up to 100 words and specific to academics), as well as a question about a significant challenge that you've faced, (up to 250 words), and three others. Lots of thought will need to go into these!

Universal Application (www.universalcollgeapp.com):

The Universal Application only serves about 34 schools at this point. It is very similar to the Commonapp and is free to create an account, but has an open ended 650-word personal statement (or essay). There is also a place to put a link to work that you've done. This can be writing, musical talent, etc. It is free so it doesn't come with the added cost of SlideRoom on the Commonapp so that might be a reason to use this application. The downside is the small number of member schools that will accept this application. When researching colleges you should look to see which application would be the best for all the schools to which you are applying.

Coalition Application (www.coalitionforcollegeaccess.org)

The Coalition Application is the newest platform and has 90 member schools. All of the members are committed to serving underrepresented students, providing substantial financial aid and keeping graduation rates reasonable. This platform allows for students to collect items that might be helpful in the college application process in a virtual locker. Items might be a graded paper that is especially well written or even a draft of your college essay. Speaking of the essay, there are five prompts for Coalition Application. One is a topic of your choice prompt. There are also prompts that are similar to the Commonapp and a couple that are completely different. There isn't a hard word limit on the essay, but the application suggests that essays should be no more than 550 words. The schools that require supplemental essays on the Commonapp will also require them with this application.

So, who should be using this platform? Some of the schools using the Coalition Application have decided to go exclusively with this application. At this time, there are only a few that are exclusive, but more could decide to go this way in the future. This application rolled out for the 2016-17 application season so I think we will know more after a year or two.

ZeeMee (www.zeemee.com):

ZeeMee is not an application platform, but a new and free supplement that is partnered with over 200 schools. It is a way for students to tell their story in a different way. You can put pictures of projects or videos on ZeeMee. There is also an optional video introduction that a student can produce, (a smartphone is fine for this), to tell the colleges a bit more about himself. The partnered colleges will have a specific spot to link your account within the application platform, but if you'd like to link to colleges that aren't members you can add your link to the additional information section on the Commonapp or other applications. If the schools aren't partners you can't be sure that they will look at your link if you add it to the application, but they might.

A student who I'm working with has a beautifully written and descriptive essay about a project that he had done. He is using ZeeMee to provide images to go with his descriptions of furniture that he had built from logs that had been submerged in a lake for years.

Students can also use ZeeMee to add more information about their activities. For example, they can add a video of a game winning goal in a soccer game or their part in a play. It's definitely for students who want a creative way to make their application more complete.

ZeeMee is fairly new so time will tell if this becomes something that more schools are looking for.

1. Is the Commonapp the best application for me?
2. How important is it to open a ZeeMee account?
3. Should I upload a resume?
4. If I use two different applications can I use the same essay?

Chapter Sixteen

Dreaded Deadlines

Deadlines are so important in college admissions. It's not like high school where you may be able to talk your way into an extra day or two for an assignment. In college admissions every application is time-stamped when it is received. This could be the difference between having your application considered for early decision or early action. It could also be the difference between getting a scholarship or not. Deadlines are nothing to mess with and since most applications are submitted online you need to give yourself some time for technical difficulties. There are several ways to apply and you need to carefully consider which plan will work best for you. Deadlines will differ with each school so check carefully.

Early Decision (ED)

This plan is for students who absolutely know that they have one and only one match for their perfect college experience. These deadlines are the typically the earliest that you will find. The majority of schools that offer an early decision deadline are very selective, including the Ivies.

The upside to applying early decision is that you will hear about your decision in December instead of March or even as late as April 1. The downside is that admission is binding and you, (and your parents), agree that you will go to this school if accepted. You will not have an opportunity to compare financial aid packages and the only ethical way to get out of this contract is to go through a process where you can prove that you can't afford to attend. If you are counting on financial aid for college this is a very tough way to apply.

Even schools that meet 100% of your financial need, like MIT and Harvard, might not give you enough aid to attend. There is more information about financial aid in another chapter. You can apply to other colleges, (regular decision only), while you are waiting to hear from your early decision college, but if you are accepted to your ED school you must withdraw all other applications. Many schools have EDI and EDII plans with deadlines that are about a month apart.

Some students believe that they will have a better chance of getting into a highly selective school by applying early. There are always debates about this. It may be that more highly qualified candidates are applying early and that is why it seems like chances to get accepted are higher with early decision. It really makes sense to apply when your application is at its absolute best. It doesn't make any sense to rush it!

Early Action (EA)

Early action is a non-binding plan that allows students to apply early and find out early while still giving students the option of waiting until National Decision Day, which is May 1st, to decide where they will be going. This plan gives students the opportunity to compare financial aid packages. Again, you don't want to apply early if your application isn't at its best. Is your testing done? Will your first semester grades help your application? These are things to think about.

Regular Decision (RD)

This is just what it sounds like. This is the decision plan with the latest deadline, but be sure to note that there is a hard deadline for this plan. This gives you a bit more time to work on your application to make it as strong as possible.

Rolling Admissions (RA)

Rolling admissions plans are most common in state schools and certainly not all state schools so be sure to check on this. With rolling admissions you can basically apply at any time-even the summer before you plan to enroll. The problem with waiting is that you might not get into your major if it's already full and you may not get any scholarship money if it's already been distributed to other students. Many schools with rolling admissions will have a priority deadline that isn't a hard deadline, but is a deadline for scholarship consideration. After that deadline scholarship money is only awarded based on availability.

Restricted Early Action (REA)

This plan is used by highly selective colleges and differs by college. It is non-binding, but you can't apply early action/decision to any other school. The exception to this may be your state university, but again, it varies by institution.

I will talk about financial aid separately, but it's important to note that all schools have financial aid deadlines as well as application deadlines and they aren't always the same. You need to do your research and keep track of all your deadlines!

1. Should I apply early decision or early action?
2. Why are the deadlines so early in my senior year?
3. Will I have a better chance if I apply early decision?

Chapter Seventeen

Scholarships and Financial Aid

This might be the most read chapter of the book. College is expensive and scholarships and grants provide money that doesn't have to be paid back. Every dollar that you get in scholarships is potentially a dollar that you don't have to borrow, (and pay back with interest).

Typically, the biggest scholarship that you receive will be from one of the colleges that accepts you. This season, I've heard about scholarships at the eight thousand dollar level at an in-state school, which is just a few hundred dollars less than full tuition, to $21,000 at a private non-profit university, which is almost half the cost of tuition and fees. Many of the school scholarships don't even require an additional application or essay and the qualifications (usually GPA and sometimes test scores) can often be found on the website. Having said that, many schools also have additional scholarships that you will need to qualify for and apply to. You should be able to find these right in the financial aid section of the college website. These special scholarships may have deadlines or require you to apply early action so be sure to check that when you are planning.

There are also a number of grants available for need-based students. The Federal Government provides Pell Grants based on need as determined by your FAFSA. There may also be state grants available to you so make sure to check this out or ask guidance for more information on what you might qualify for.

Aside from scholarships that are awarded by colleges, there are several other ways to gain scholarship money. There are local, state and national scholarships to which you can, and probably should, apply. How many scholarships you apply to will be determined by your level of need, amount of free time and, frankly, your energy level and drive. Scholarships are really helpful in the college process and they are really fun and self-affirming when you get one. There are scholarships that are basically a monthly giveaway and totally determined by luck as well as scholarships that require essays, a copy of your transcript and perhaps letters of recommendation.

Local scholarships are a great place to start. These don't tend to be a ton of money, but they are usually easy to apply for and every little bit counts. If you get a $100 scholarship for five minutes of work than that's a pretty good return on investment of your time! Look for these in your community. They might be at the local credit union or your parent's place of employment. Check your high school website as local scholarships are often listed there. Sometimes high schools will have a bunch of local scholarships that they are charged with distributing each year. Often all that is required is filling out a form with your pertinent information. It always amazed me how many students didn't bother to spend a few minutes to fill out this form. It's no fun sitting at awards night in June and not getting anything because you didn't take the time to fill something out. It might also make your parents super mad!

You also might be able to find scholarships on the state level. Because you are competing with more students these might be harder to get, but they are probably also more money. Again, these might be listed on guidance pages on school websites or your state may have a non-profit agency that has scholarship information available.

There are several scholarship search engines to help you sort out the national scholarships. You will need to sign up with an email address, but they can customize your search so that you don't have to look at a bunch of scholarships that are not relevant to you. Be prepared to get a lot of emails from colleges and these search engines. I've looked at several of these and they seem to have a lot of the same scholarships so I wouldn't sign up for more than one or you will be spending all your time sorting through the same information. There are also scholarship apps for your devices and some are free. Here are some of the more popular scholarship search engines:

www.fastweb.com

www.scholarship.com

www.bigfuture.collegeboard.org/scholarship-search

www.chegg.com

www.zinch

I have a few last words on scholarships and searches. Never pay for a scholarship application, be organized and mindful of deadlines and don't let yourself get overwhelmed.

Financial Aid

The way that financial aid works in the US is under the assumption that your parents will help you pay for college. Whether this is the case or not, they will need to participate in helping you with the forms, (by filling them out or giving you access to their financial information). There are a couple of exceptions, but most college going students will need their parents tax info if they want to apply for aid.

There are basically two types of financial aid. There is need based aid, which is just what it sounds like. It is in place to help meet the need a family might have when paying for college and there is merit based aid, which is based on student achievement.

Need Based Aid

Need is determined by the Free Application for Federal Student Aid (FAFSA). You will input your information and will get a Student Aid Report (SAR), which will tell you how much your family can afford to pay for college in the form of an Expected Family Contribution (EFC) based on the answers to the questions regarding income and assets. There are other factors like the age of the oldest parent and how many kids in the family will be in college. It is quite common that people don't agree with the figure of how much a family can pay each year. To get back an EFC of $40,000 per year can be a bit alarming! Disagreeing with your financial aid is a topic for later.

You can now access this online form as early as October of your senior year and you can use tax reports from the year that began in January of your sophomore year. The IRS has a data retrieval tool (DRT) that makes it very easy to get this information. To file the FAFSA you will need to send the information to at least one school and can send it to up to ten for free. If you have more than ten schools it gets tricky, but is not impossible as long as you file in advance of the financial aid deadlines.

To file the form, you and one parent will need to get an FSA ID. Here is a blog post that I wrote after a financial aid bootcamp that I attended before the new opening date for the FAFSA was implemented in 2016:

You may have heard that the Free Application for Federal Student Aid (FAFSA) is opening early this year... and from now on. What does this mean? To receive need-based financial aid for college all students will need to fill out the FAFSA. Students who may not be eligible for need-based aid, but want to take advantage of Federal loans, and in some cases, merit aid, will also need to fill out the FAFSA. Beginning this year, the FAFSA will open on October 1. This is three months earlier than in the past. What will this mean? It's hard to say. Will students get their financial aid reports from schools earlier? Time will tell. So, what do you need to do? You can't file for the FAFSA until October 1, but you can make sure that your, (and your parents), 2015 tax returns are all done and filed. You can also get your FSA ID.

What is this FSA ID that you speak of? Good question. The FSA ID is a way to electronically sign your FAFSA and also a way to gain access to other important financial aid forms, (think loans). Every student who is applying for financial aid for college should have a FSA ID....and they will need one of their parents to have an FSA ID as well. You, and a parent, can get your FSA IDs by going to www.fsaid.ed.gov . You will need social security numbers and birth dates to get an ID. It is recommended for parents, and really necessary for students, to use an email address, one for each of you, that you will have access to until your student loans are paid. This is a great time to come up with a gmail address that you can use for college applications and shouldn't be anything that is ridiculous like partygrl@gmail.com. I don't know if this is taken, but just don't go there! Students and parents cannot share an email address when there are setting up separate FSA IDs.

If your parents have older kids who have gone through the financial aid process, they may already have a PIN number. If they remember what it is, they can merge it with the new FSA ID system. If the PIN number system means nothing to you then just focus on the FSA ID. This is what you need to have in 2016 and beyond.

So, why would you get your ID now if you don't need to file until October? Good question. The answer is because whatever you can do now you won't have to do later when you are worried about college applications. It is also something that needs to be done correctly so if you have more time and concentration now then you might have two hours before a financial aid deadline then I would suggest that you take advantage of that. When applying for your FSA ID be sure to read the instructions and make sure that all the info is correct. You only have one SS# so make sure that you are accurate in entering it!

One other thing to think about. You will have an opportunity to have your email verified. This can be very helpful later if you don't remember your user name and password (do you have a system to keep track of usernames and passwords? This might be a good time to start). By verifying your email....and this is the basic gmail that doesn't suggest to colleges anything about your social life, it will be a lot easier to get into your account should you forget your user name, password, or choose to change your security questions. To get your email verified, you will need to put in your email and then retrieve a code from said email, within ten minutes or so, and enter this code. Once this is done you are all good. Your social security # will be linked with this email and you will have easy access to your information for years to come.

It may not seem like much, but believe me, you will be happy that you have done this later. Fall of senior year is incredibly busy with applications, AP classes, and leadership obligations. By doing this now it will be so very easy to apply for financial aid and complete the FAFSA come Oct. 1. One last word on financial aid-check all your deadlines. Know when your first deadline is and make sure that you file for maximum considerations for aid. Also, know if you need to file the Profile. This separate financial aid application (owned by Collegeboard) often has different deadlines. Preparing now will save you lots of angst (SAT word?) later!

If you don't think that you will get any financial aid and don't want to bother with filling out the FAFSA you need to think about two things. Do you want/need Federal loans to pay for college? Do any of your schools require you to fill out the FAFSA before they will consider you for merit money? If you don't need loans or merit money it is still a good idea to file the FAFSA in case something changes in the future. There are schools that won't let you file in later years if you didn't file your freshman year. The FAFSA can be found at www.fafsa.gov and you should never pay someone to file the FAFSA for you.

There are some schools that require the FAFSA, but also require another, more complex, form called the CSS Profile, or known as just the Profile in some financial aid offices. The CSS Profile is owned by CollegeBoard and can be linked from their site as well as many financial aid pages on college sites. The CSS Profile looks at things that the FAFSA doesn't, like the value of your primary home and if your parents own a business. The colleges that require the CSS Profile are mostly highly selective, private and non-profit liberal arts colleges. The CSS Profile also opens in October and uses the same tax year as the FAFSA, but deadlines may be different so beware and be diligent with keeping track of all your deadlines. The CSS Profile also charges you per school to send your information.

Net Price Calculator

Every school that receives Federal money has to have a Net Price Calculator on their website. I mentioned this earlier and noted that some of these tools are better than others and it also matters how accurate the information is that you use. CollegeBoard has a Net Price Calculator on its site that has almost 220 schools associated with it. This is nice because you can save the information in one place, but if you are looking at a school that is not using the CollegeBoard NPC you can use the calculator on the school website. This is a great place to start when trying to figure out what you might get from schools for aid. Some Net Price Calculators will ask for grades and scores and will factor in potential merit money.

Once need is established through the FAFSA and maybe the CSS Profile it's up to schools to decide if they will try to help you meet this need. Some schools will only meet 60% of need while others, like Harvard and MIT will meet full need. Again, what your financial aid numbers give you for need and what you think your need is may be wildly different. In any case, it's always a good idea to look at the percentage of need that schools meet to get an idea of what your aid package might look like.

Merit Aid or Money

Merit money is money that a student might get based on achievements or talents. It could be a scholarship for excellent (or sometimes just mediocre) grades and test scores or it could come in the form of an athletic scholarship.

To be clear, only NCAA Division I and II schools can offer athletic scholarships and many college athletes are not receiving any scholarship at all. If you think you can compete at the higher levels and want to try for an athletic scholarship you should be contacting coaches and you will need to register with the NCAA clearinghouse at www.eligibilitycenter.org.

The US Service Academies are a great deal for students who are interested in serving our country. Applying to them is quite complicated and you must start early. There are other books available for students and families interested in this avenue.

Let's get back to merit money. Some colleges will give more merit money than others. Earlier, I wrote about discount rates, which helps to figure out which schools put more money into scholarships. Sometimes you can get an idea of what you might expect for merit money from the financial aid websites of the schools you are considering. Some will break down what the qualifications are for the different levels of scholarship that they offer. As I mentioned in the need based aid section, some schools will ask for students to fill out the FAFSA to be considered for merit money so please do your research.

1. How do I know which schools give the most money?
2. Will you help me with my FAFSA?

Chapter Eighteen

The Acceptance Letter (and other options)

Applications are in and the waiting is almost over. Soon application decisions will be coming to students everywhere. For students who applied early there are generally three options and these decisions are often made before the first of the year. They may be accepted, (yay), denied, or deferred. Students who apply regular decision won't get deferred, but they might get put on a waitlist. These decisions will be made known to students in the spring. Usually before the first of April.

Something that has changed over the last few years is that students are hearing about their acceptances via email. You will still (in most cases) get a letter in the mail, but the first place you might see whether or not you've been accepted to a school is in your inbox. Many schools are asking students who apply to open a portal, which is used for communication with the admissions office and the financial aid office. You will get this notification via the email you used on your application so be sure to check for these important emails and follow the instructions for setting up the portals. Should you decide to attend a school that asks that you set up a portal you will be getting a lot of important info this way.

This is not always the smoothest transaction. In 2016, a lot of students who applied early action to Tulane received financial aid or scholarship information before they were officially accepted. This caused a lot of confusion and anxiety. This is probably because the financial aid and admissions offices don't talk to each other. Tulane is committed to meeting over 90% of student need and perhaps 2016 was a tough year for them with new FAFSA filing date. In any case, it's really important to look for emails and follow the instructions. In a case like this where the admission decision is unclear it might make sense to call, or ask your counselor to call, admissions to see what is going on.

If you didn't get accepted or denied in the early round of admission decisions you most likely got deferred, (this should be clearly stated in your email or letter). This just means that your application will be considered again in the next round when the regular decision applications are being read. It means that you are a strong enough candidate to keep in consideration, but you didn't make the first cut. It's certainly not as exciting as getting an acceptance letter, but the school is still interested enough to keep you around a bit longer. If you are deferred from a binding early decision application then it means that it's time to get other applications out there. You will no longer be bound to that school should they accept you in the next round. It's a bummer if this is your first choice school, but you need to keep moving forward with applications and planning for your future.

Schools also use waitlists to manage enrollment and you may find yourself sitting on one. What can you do when this happens? First, you have to realize that if this is your dream school then your dream has not died. You haven't been accepted and cannot claim a seat in the next class, but if the school doesn't get enough students to attend then they will turn to the waitlist. If you find yourself sitting here there are a few things that you should do. You can call the school to see how often they turn to the waitlist and when they do use the waitlist, what is the average number of students that move into the incoming class. It also helps to know how long the list is. They won't be able to give you a number of where you fall on the list because they will be looking for certain things to fill the incoming class. For example-if it is a school that tries to keep a 50/50 ratio between males and females and way more females deposit at the school, (letting the school know their intention to attend), but the school didn't get enough males to fill all the seats in the class then they will go to the waitlist, but will most likely only look for males to gain balance in the class.

What you can do if you are waitlisted and are still very interested in attending this school is to let them know that you would attend if accepted, (only if this is true). You can also let them know of any updates that would make your application more attractive and competitive-like awards, grades or test scores. Your school counselor should be able to help you out with this.

You should also evaluate the schools where you were admitted. These schools were on your list for a reason and are probably still very good options for you. You will most likely need to make a deposit way before you will hear from your waitlist school. At this point a lot of students will just commit to the new school and let the waitlist school go. Sometimes it's as late as August before students are plucked off the waitlist. This is a decision that you have to make. Years ago, I worked with a student who, on paper, was the perfect candidate for a small liberal arts school in Pennsylvania. I called the school on his behalf and was told that his best shot at getting off the waitlist was to let the school know that he would be willing to wait until August before he might know if he was offered a seat in the class. He, very smartly in my opinion, let that school go, committed to another school and had a great experience. Once he let the school where he was on the waitlist go, he was free to explore the opportunities at the school where he ended up. It was actually a relief for him to make this decision, but I'll bet that he spent a week agonizing over what might have been.

The last option is an outright denial. This is very disappointing to most students even if the school was way down on their list. It hurts to be denied and it's worth spending a small amount of time indulging in your feelings of rejection. After that short period of time you need to pull yourself up and prepare for your future-at another school. There are many reasons that you may find yourself denied admission at a college or university. Maybe you really weren't a strong candidate or maybe you applied in a year where there were just too many great candidates and some had to be denied. If you believe that, 'everything happens for a reason,' then maybe you just weren't meant to attend that school. If this isn't your personal philosophy it really doesn't matter. The most important thing is that you move on and commit to another, probably, equally great school.

National decision day is May 1 and schools should not ask you to send in a deposit before that date. There may be instances where schools will suggest that you deposit early especially if housing is at a premium and not guaranteed. In these cases they will often refund your deposit if you change your mind before May 1.

You should have at least a month to go over your financial aid packages and, if possible, attend accepted student days, at the schools that you are considering. It is widely frowned upon to double deposit (or send in deposits to hold your place at more than one school). The only time that you could or should do this is in the case of the waitlist if you are holding out for a spot.

Once you do make a decision on where to deposit you should send an email to the other schools that accepted you so that they can manage their enrollment and perhaps work their waitlist.

1. How much is the deposit?
2. Do I need to tell a school if I want to stay on the waitlist?

Chapter Nineteen

Financial Aid Packages

Almost as important as the acceptance is the financial aid package! This could be the difference between attending a school and moving on to a different one with a better financial aid package. There are several components to a financial aid package and schools seem to each have their own way of detailing the different components. Some will add loans to the financial aid award letter, while others will leave a bigger gap and let the student decide if loans will be part of the plan. For this reason you must be very careful when disseminating the award, (or financial aid), letter.

The first thing that you want to do is figure out the Cost of Attendance, (COA). This might be done for you on the award letter or you may have to go looking for some numbers. You will need to find these fixed costs:

1. Tuition and mandatory fees for one year
2. Room and board, (if you plan to live on campus), also for one year

Fixed costs don't change, but there are also some variable costs that you will need to account for when calculating the COA. These costs might be:

1. Books and supplies
2. Travel. This is for travel to and from school, not study abroad
3. Health insurance if you aren't on your parents' plan
4. Fun budget. You're going to want to go to the movies so plan for it here, (this can also go under books and supplies to make it simple)

If you take your fixed costs and add your variable costs you will have your total COA.

Next you will want to look for any free money. This comes in the form of scholarships from the college and grants. Grants are typically need-based, while scholarships are typically merit based, (but, I did already mention that some schools require financial aid info to award merit money). Neither of these awards need to be paid back, (that's why they are free), but the amounts will vary from student to student based on need and merit.

There are grants from the institution itself, the federal government, (Pell Grants), and perhaps your state. You will want to add the total of all your grants to the total scholarship number. You will then subtract your free money from the COA to obtain your net price. Once you have your net price you will be able to figure out how much additional money you will need to provide for a year at the college.

You may see things like work study and federal loans in your package. These should be considered money that has to be paid back. Work-study doesn't have to be paid back, but you do have to work for it.

Every school has their own way of presenting aid awards so you need to separate out the different parts of the award to be able to compare apples to apples. For this reason, I have created a worksheet that compares what the total out-of-pocket cost to the family will be when all is said and done.

Financial Aid Comparison Worksheet

	Example	A	B	C
Tuition & mandatory fees	10,628			
Room and Board	10,164			
Books, supplies & misc	2,000			
Travel	1,200			
Total COA	23,992			
Free Money				
Total of all grants	-			
School Scholarships	4,000			
	19,992			

*Subtract free money from COA to get Net Price

Work-study	1,800			
Federal loans	-			
PLUS loans	-			
Private loans	-			
Out of pocket cost	18,192			

This example assumes no loans are needed or wanted, but once you get the out of pocket cost you can go back and plug in some numbers for loans. It also assumes that this student received work-study, which probably doesn't add up with my other assumptions, but lots of students do get work-study so I've added it in. The work-study number is the maximum amount of money you are eligible to receive under that program and is determined by the school and could vary from package to package.

Once you figure out which school is offering the best deal then you can figure out how you will pay. It may also be that you will choose not to attend the school that gives you the best deal, but with the comparison tool you will know what's on the table for each school. Many schools offer payment plans. These may not be monthly, but perhaps four payments per semester. I've also heard of a family who used a reward credit card to make payments. This is only a good idea if you can pay that balance off each month. I haven't done any specific research, but I'm guessing you can get a better rate on a student loan than you may be paying on a credit card.

Speaking of loans-there are several options. The federal government offers several different loans:

- **Direct-subsidized loan.** This is need based and interest doesn't accrue until after you graduate.
- **Direct-unsubsidized loan.** This is not need based and the interest will accrue beginning when the money is distributed.
- **Federal Perkins loan.** These aren't offered at all schools because essentially the school is the lender. This is need based.
- **Federal Direct PLUS loan.** This loan is for parents and a credit check is necessary.
- **Private loans.** These can be found at banks, credit unions and other financial institutions. Sometimes the college will list lenders that other students have used, but they aren't

connected in any way with the school. These aren't controlled by the federal government and should be looked at carefully-make sure to compare rates and repayment programs.

For more information on federal loans you can go to www.studentaid.ed.gov. If you have questions you can always talk with the financial aid office at each school or check with your school counselor for help.

If you believe that you have circumstances that the financial aid office has not taken into consideration in your award you can ask for a review. Some instances of this might be a parent's loss of a job, taking care of relatives and loss of child support. You can ask for work study if you weren't offered it, but you should do this early before all the work study money is gone. You can also ask for Stafford loans if they aren't listed on your award letter.

I left private scholarships off the comparison tool for two reasons. First, you may not know about them yet and second, they may not change the amount that a family is expected to pay. Some schools will reduce their grant or scholarship money when you tell them about a private scholarship. But you still need to tell them.

Stacking scholarships is when a student qualifies for two or more scholarships at a school. Some schools will give the student both scholarships and some will only award the larger of the two. This is a good thing to put on your list of things to research especially if you think that you might qualify for multiple scholarships.

1. What is a good scholarship amount?
2. When will I get my financial aid letter?
3. I don't want any loans-where should I go to school?

Chapter Twenty

Accepted Students Days (and other things to help you decide)

As I've written, you should have all your acceptances by around April 1. This gives you at least a month to make a decision and send in your deposit. This is a busy month and you might be preparing for upcoming AP exams in May, but you need to spend some time really evaluating your college choices. The earlier that you are accepted the sooner you can put some of the following ideas into practice.

A lot of colleges will host accepted student days in the spring. These are basically open houses for students who have been accepted and give the students access to professors, departments and students, (both current and prospective). This is a great way to get on campus one more time and make sure that everything you loved about the school is still relevant to you. You can also make an appointment with financial aid if you have any questions about your financial aid package. I really can't stress enough how important this extra visit is. If you weren't able to get on campus when you were applying then it's really important to get on campus now unless it's financially impossible and the college is across the country. Nothing replaces the feel of being on a campus. Promotional videos on the website are just that, promotional.

You might also have a chance to spend a night and attend a class or two. This is a great way to 'try-on' a school. Make sure that you schedule these in advance. If the school doesn't offer this then perhaps you have a friend who attends the school and can spend some quality time there by visiting your friend. There is also this thing called a gut-check. This is when you just have to listen to your gut about a school. The assumption here is that you will know if it's a good fit, (or not), by listening to your gut.

The way the whole college thing works is that first you go out and find schools that you like or even love. These schools will be happy that you are so interested and may send you lots of love in the form of emails or printed materials. Then you apply. The ball is in their court and you just hang around doing senior year things until you hear back from these lovely schools. It can feel like forever and you are suddenly missing the daily deluge from your mailman. Once you are accepted the ball is back in your court and emails and printed materials will begin to appear, once again. These emails and postcards will tell you of all the wonderful things that are going on at school X. They have accepted you, (and many others), and really want you to deposit at their school. It's a delicate, albeit stressful, dance and emotions can be like a roller coaster.

You may change your mind several times about which college is your first choice. One day it may be strictly a financial decision and another it may be because the basketball team is in March madness and that looks like it would be super fun to be part of. You look great in their colors, right? Sometimes you might be thinking more seriously about your education and what programs a certain college offers and other times you may be dreaming of the world renowned study abroad program in New Zealand at a totally different college that has a lousy basketball team. This is perfectly normal, but you do have to choose one and only one.

I think the very best way to get a really good feel is to get back on campus when students are there. I was touring Clark University in Worcester, Mass. earlier this year and was walking through a dorm with a family on my tour. There were several girls sitting on the floor of the hallway chatting and we had to walk over and through them. They stopped talking and started almost chanting, "Come to Clark" to the high school senior girl who was on my tour. I'm sure that this made her feel welcome. I have no idea where she will end up, but she had the experience of seeing friendly students who were speaking directly to her. I think the girls were freshmen and, clearly, they were proud of their school! If you can't make an accepted students event then just get back on campus. It can be either formal where you might meet with a professor or it can be informal where you go to the dining hall and have a meal. If you go with a friend make sure that you are doing what you went there to do. Don't just chat with your friend about weekend plans- seek out students and connect with them. Students are almost always happy to talk with prospectives.

There are other things that you can do to connect with colleges that have accepted you. Check them out on Facebook if you haven't already. Be sure to 'like' the college page. Often there will be open Facebook groups for accepted students-you should definitely join. The group will usually be named something like class of 20xx- whatever your college graduation year will be. Many students will turn to this page once they deposit at a school and meet kids even before orientation. For now, you just want to see what kids are talking about. Many of these kids may have already decided and will be very excited about their choice. This excitement is contagious.

You can and should follow your school on Instagram. Once you follow the school you may find current students and you can follow them as well. You will see pretty posts of snowfall or sunsets over the pond. You may also see students prepping for a night out. You should be able to get an idea of student life from various forms of social media. Don't forget Twitter-140 characters can tell you a lot. Don't be too alarmed if it's finals time and you are seeing a lot of stressed out tweets. I'm pretty sure this happens at every school during every finals period.

Perusing the website is also a way to get more familiar with your choices. You can take the virtual tour again and check the course catalog to see what classes you might like to take. You can look at any core requirements and be sure that they are in line with your academic goals. If a school has a fluency requirement in a foreign language and you hate taking foreign language you might want to eliminate that school. You probably wouldn't have applied in the first place, but it may have been something that you missed for some reason. It's better to find out now rather than when you are sitting in French 1 in the fall.

If you know what you want to study in college you can connect with a professor in that department if you have any questions about the academics. You can also ask if you can be connected with a student in that major to get the real deal. The same goes for a club- for example if you want to play club baseball you can ask to be connected with a student who is on the club team. Ask how difficult it is to balance study and play or any questions you might have.

If you are contemplating the Honors College or program at a school it would be a really good idea to connect with an honors student to see how that program works. Does she live in honors housing? Is it an intense program? Does she only take one honors class per semester? How much class discussion is involved, (probably a lot, by the way)?

A lot of colleges have all freshmen read the same book over the summer and use it for discussion in their first year experience class first semester. See if you can find out what they will be reading at each college. I'm not suggesting that you pick a college based on a book, but it might give you just a bit more insight to the culture of the school. It's quite possible that it hasn't been decided yet so perhaps you can see what they read last year.

All these little pieces of information should help to get you really familiar with the college choices that you have. If you had to eliminate a college because the financials just didn't work please don't torture yourself with any of these strategies. Let that one go and move on.

College really is more than a name. It's what you make of it so do your research to find the best academic, social and financial fit for YOU.

1. Do I really have to do another college visit?
2. Do I have to contact a professor?

Chapter Twenty-One

Honors Colleges and Programs

What are honors colleges and are they for me? These programs are generally offered to the top students and come with benefits like early class registration. Some colleges have special honors housing. Below is part of a blog that I wrote about honors colleges at large state universities. Some smaller liberal arts colleges have some sort of honors programs. This would be something to research if you are interested in a more challenging course of study.

Honors Colleges have been getting a lot of press lately because they can be a more affordable way for academically excellent students to have the experience of a small liberal arts college at a large public university, (with in-state or significantly lower tuition). Honors Colleges are not a new thing, in fact the Honors College at the University of Maine has been around since the 1930's! Some have set criteria for admission or even a separate application with additional essay. This blog will explore how the Honors College works at the University of Maine in Orono, Maine, specifically. If you are interested in other Honors Colleges, I'm sure that you can find info on their websites or on a visit to the school.

The University of Maine at Orono, or UMaine as it will be referred to here, has had an Honors College for years. Currently, there are about 800 students involved in the program. Each of these students is also studying in one of the other colleges at the university, (liberal arts & sciences, engineering, business-you get the picture). Honors College at UMaine is a 24-27 credit program that is an inter-disciplinary approach which enriches the learning that is happening within a students major.

So how do you get into this program that offers access to professors, fellowship opportunities, study abroad programs, honors housing and the opportunity to do a senior thesis or Capstone? At UMaine, the top 20% of the incoming class are invited to join the Honors College. It's completely up to the student whether she takes advantage of this opportunity. There is not a separate application, (no additional essays), and there aren't clear criteria for admission to the Honors College. The top 20% takes into account SAT/ACT scores and high school GPA and these variables change every year based on the make-up of the admitted class. If you are admitted early you will have to wait to find out about admission to the honors college-they want to review applications received through their preferred regular application deadline of 2/1.

Students typically take one honors class per semester. These classes often count toward the student's general education requirements for graduation so these aren't 'extra' classes. Honors classes will be more discussion based due to the small size, (typically between 8-14 students). To graduate with honors a student must complete the requirements of the program and have a 3.3 GPA.

Honors colleges can be a great way to make a big school feel smaller and you will have a built in community. You can leave the honors college if your other coursework is overwhelming and many students who are in really intense majors, like engineering, feel that they don't have time to pursue honors college. They will have a community from the beginning due to the nature of their majors so the community benefit may not be a draw like it could be with someone studying something in the liberal arts area.

1. What happens if I get into the Honors College and don't want to do it?
2. Can I drop out if I don't like it or it's too hard?

Chapter Twenty-Two

Orientation

College orientations come in many shapes and sizes. Some are very short and informative, while others take place over days and may even include team-building like adventures.

They are often a time to pick classes for first semester freshman year and a way to begin to get to know your new home for the next four years.

Students will meet new friends that they may or may not keep for the next four years, but will at least have a friendly face or two when they get to campus in August or September.

Some students will make a connection with someone and choose to be freshman roommates. Others will choose someone, without as much of a connection, to be a freshman roommate because the known, (albeit not for very long), is better than the unknown.

There will be serious meetings and talks about things like sexual consent and date rape drugs and fun things like ice cream parties and scavenger hunts.

Some schools will have a shorter program for parents because parents need help with this big transition, too.

Some orientations are mandatory, while others are not. In any case, you should definitely put orientation on your to-do list for the summer. You will learn a lot about your new community and it will help you feel more comfortable when you settle in a month or two later.

You may be nervous about attending orientation, but the students and staff who work at orientation will do everything that they can to make you feel more comfortable. It's a great learning opportunity for you and you should get as much out of it as possible.

If you go to a big state school you will find that some students will already know lots of other students. If this school isn't in your state you will probably not know anyone at all—unless you've met some potential friends on Facebook. Even the students who seem to already have a group of friends are eager to meet new ones so don't be afraid to talk to others.

1. What if my parents can't come? Is that OK?
2. Why is orientation mandatory at some schools?

Chapter Twenty-Three

Getting Ready to Fly

By the time summer rolls around and graduation is in the rear view mirror you will be thinking about the future and your next big step. This is an interesting time for everyone in the family.

I've talked to parents whose emotions swing from wanting to kick their kids out of the house to wanting to hold on to them forever. It really just depends on the day. On some days parents feel that drop-off day will never come and on others they feel like they can't possibly get everything done before their chick flies the nest. All while trying to create family memories that will sustain everyone until fall break or Thanksgiving. Parents and students, alike, have had a whole year of lasts-last football game, last winter concert and more, but it often feels that a year isn't time enough for this huge transition. It's not just the recent graduate that will be embarking on a new life, but the family structure will take on a new and different dynamic. It's not a bad thing it's just a different thing. If the student leaving creates an empty nest then that is a whole different situation. A void that parents will learn to fill, but may seem impossible until the student actually leaves. There will be a learning curve for everyone-even the family dog who won't understand where his sleeping buddy went or why he left.

Students high off graduation, prom and the crazy last week of high school will have to navigate this new terrain with care. You may be working to save money to pay for school and dealing with demanding bosses while trying to be home for as many family dinners as mom can get you to agree to. This might be the first real job that you've had so you may be adjusting to what it feels like to work five days a week. You probably won't have to do much adjusting to a weekly paycheck.

You also want to spend every waking moment with friends.....until you don't. Students headed to college for the first time are often feeling tugged in many directions. It may feel like everyone wants a piece of you and that's an uncomfortable feeling. You may be constantly with friends until it sinks in that you won't have this constant access when everyone goes off to school. You may then take some time for yourself to process what it means to leave everything comfortable behind for a new life. Summer will seem incredibly long at times and super short at others.

You may start trying to meet people from your new community on Facebook or other social media sites. You may be interacting with all sorts of new people and may even feel that your own family and hometown are lame, (horrors). This is all normal. Going off to college is both exciting and terrifying and you need to experience both.

There may also be the question of what you and your significant other will do. Do you do the long distance thing or just break up now and have some time to get over it before even stepping on campus. You can Google the subject to see what others have to say, but ultimately it will be between you and your high school love. I will give you some things to think about, but no one can really tell you what to do. Will you date others if you stay together? Will you commit to FaceTiming at a certain time each week? Will you feel that you are missing out on something if you go to college and are in a relationship? Is seeing other people an experience that you'd like to have? Most likely this will be a hard conversation no matter what you decide to do.

If your college has asked you to read a book over the summer to discuss in your first year experience class then you need to make time to do this. You know that you want to start college off on the right foot, but who wants to read, This I Believe, which was the Bates College common read for the class of 2020. You've already done so much self-reflection, after all. Actually, this sounds like a pretty good book, but still, you might rather reread one of the Harry Potter books in your downtime.

There is also the business of packing. You will need to bring a whole bunch of stuff, but will most likely be sharing a small room with very little storage space. What do you need bring in August and what can be saved for bringing back after a break are things that need to be sorted out. Will you be close enough to have your parents run your winter boots over to before the extremely early October snowstorm? If not, you need to gamble on whether you can make it until Thanksgiving before cluttering your dorm room with clunky, yet necessary, outerwear. If you are headed to Florida for college you are in better shape as flip flops take up much less room than Bean boots. Speaking of boots-is your new campus a cowboy boot type of campus and if not will you risk the possible fashion faux pas by bringing yours?

If you are going to college in Florida from one of our winter loving states will you be driving or flying? Flying takes college packing to a whole different dimension! Can you handle the overweight and extra baggage fees? Can you handle the three suitcases when you land in Florida? Will mom have time to overnight you items that you forgot? Lots to consider here. Will you be able to store some stuff when you leave in May to go home for the summer? Suddenly, the thought of filling the family SUV with all your possessions seems more appealing.

Do you know who your roommate is and will you try to coordinate dorm décor with her? Those Bed Bath and Beyond dorm rooms are so well done-will yours look like that? Also, how much money do you want to spend to make sure that you and your roommate have matching trash cans? If you have older friends who have been through this already it might make sense to talk with them.

You may also be thinking about what things from high school you want to bring to your new life. Will you actually wear your letter jacket with the big C for captain and all the pins that you earned for playing varsity? Some kids do and others don't-it's really just another thing that you need to think about. What about your collection of stuffed animals? Why did you ever let your grandmother know that you liked elephants? Now you have approximately 100 of them. Will your roommate think this is weird? Is this the impression you want to make?

What about the picture collage with all your BFFs from high school? With this be comforting to you or will it make you miss them more?

Some moms get a little crazy with dorm decoration and want to buy everything you might possibly need. Is it better to just let mom take over the decorating and purchasing? It's always better to have this conversation before the Amazon boxes start rolling in. Maybe give mom the power to take care of the bedding if you don't care-you might just want to give her some idea of your never ever color that must be avoided at all costs!

Most colleges will provide a suggested list of things to bring, but even this is probably too much. A first aid kit is a good idea and we wished that we had a tool kit when we dropped our oldest off and the beds were bunked and needed to be lofted. Some mom or dad on his floor was smart enough to bring that tool kit, but did anyone ever use it again? What about a bathrobe, (probably not for a guy), and how many towels, (how often will you do laundry and how many times can you use a towel between washings)? Last year, one of my Facebook friends did something that I thought was brilliant. Instead of asking what she should bring she asked her Facebook community what item we packed for our child that was unnecessary. In my case it was a bathrobe and in my defense I thought he could use it if he went to visit a friends family over break. He never did.

If it helps at all, you will probably get to know where the local Walmart is as soon as the car is unloaded and you realize that you forgot to bring a TV or broom or area rug or... well, I think you get the picture.

1. I'm scared to go away. Is this normal?
2. I'm really excited to get out of this small town. Is this normal?

Chapter Twenty-Four

You're Here, Now What

Drop off day is over and only a few tears were shed. Suddenly you are in your new bedroom, (dorm room), and looking at the unfamiliar rug that was purchased in haste earlier in the day because the floor is ugly and hard and cold. Your roommate may or may not have arrived yet. So, what are you supposed to do?

You will probably have a hall meeting later in the day or in the next few days. You will play ice breaker games with the strangers who will become your friends, or at the very least, will be familiar faces in the dining hall.

Conventional wisdom says to leave your dorm room door open when you are inside hanging out and not trying to study. This is a good strategy as you may have a particularly gregarious floor mate who might be looking to meet as many new people as possible. You may even find two young men (or women) appear at your door on crutches, looking for sympathy and trying to meet members of the opposite sex. You know that they don't need those crutches because you recognize the letter jacket that one of them is wearing and you saw him ably walking across the quad earlier. You invite them in and learn about the room down the hall where two roommates really do need crutches. They are probably resting on their beds (in a fourth floor walk-up dorm) while these two are making the rounds with war stories and fake injuries. This is a long story and probably won't happen, but you never know what might- especially if you keep your door open!

Social Media

I have some very strong opinions surrounding social media when you get to college. Don't spend all your time watching your high school friends on social media. They may look like they are having a ball at their school. They may, in fact, be having a ball, or they could just be projecting an image to the world. During orientation you and your parents may be told to try not to have too much contact during the first six weeks. I would also add that this is a good policy with your high school friends as well. Don't spend all afternoon on FaceTime talking with your old friends. Instead you should use that time to make new friends. It really will make your transition smoother. It will also give you lots to talk about with your high school friends when you see them all over Thanksgiving.

Opportunities Outside of the Classroom

Back to what you should do on your new campus. You will also want to visit the activities fair and see what clubs you might be interested in. If you watch The Middle, you may have seen the episode where Sue goes to the activities fair and signs up for everything because you don't even have to have any talent and there are no cuts. If you are a fan of the show you will know that she had trouble with try-outs for cheerleading in high school. You really don't need to sign up for everything-in fact, you really shouldn't. It is a good idea to see if you are interested in one or two clubs or activities. Service clubs, intramural sports, student government are some options. You probably remembering hearing, on every single campus that you toured, that you can also start your own club with a few members and a faculty advisor. For now, you can see what might already be in place. Studies have shown that involved students tend to stay in school and graduate on time. Parents might be especially interested in the staying in school and graduating on time statistic!

Places of worship may try to lure you over with ice cream parties. Go ahead and have a sundae compliments of St. Joe's. You may find a time when you are looking for a place of peace or want to participate in worship. At least you will know where to go if you've already dropped in for sweet treats.

Go to Class

Going to class is the single most important thing that you can do in college. This is, after all, why you are there! If you figure out how much money each class costs you will realize that you are paying a lot of money for that seat time and a nap is not a good excuse to miss it. Plus, you may pick up tips about what might be on the next quiz by being in class and paying attention.

Time Management

The above examples deal with getting to know your new community, but the other part of college is time management and classes. College is not like high school where you need to be in one place for up to eight hours a day. You are free to move around. In fact you will probably have to move around, as it's unlikely that you will have all your classes in one building, especially your first semester. Depending on how many classes you are taking you will only be in class for about 15 hours a week. That's like two days in the high school world. This gives you a lot of time to do other things. These other things may be some of the activities that you signed up for, but you also need to factor in homework. At some highly selective schools it's not unusual to spend three hours on homework for every hour of seat time each and every week. So 15 hours a week plus 45 hours of homework is a pretty busy week with just academics. Throw in a club and a 10-hour a week work-study job and your week is pretty full.

New friends will take up some of your time. You will meet your new friends in class, in clubs and, of course, in your dorm. These freshmen friends may be your friends for life or they may just be friends that you will do things with while you are making other friends, who may become your lifelong friends. It doesn't really matter.

Take Care of Yourself and Others

Whichever kind of friend you are hanging out with when you first get to school be sure to take care of each other. I'm not going to pretend that freshmen in college spend all their time studying because they are too young to drink. You may be faced with party options and this is part of college. All I'm saying is that you need to take care of each other. Never leave a friend at a party, (no matter how cute the guy is who asks you to leave it), and be sure to ask a friend to walk you home if you want to leave or call the security office to get a ride. Also, never leave a party alone with any person that you don't know well.

The buddy system that you may have used on field trips in elementary school works equally as well in college. Especially in strange situations or if you may find yourself not thinking clearly. Never, ever, leave an open drink unattended-even if it doesn't contain alcohol. Date rape drugs are used (on both males and females) to render the person helpless and open to assault. Remember that everyone is coming to college with different backgrounds and some people might be more familiar with their tolerance for alcohol than others. Take care of each other and look out for each other. It's always better to be safe than sorry. I'm not trying to scare you. The 18-22 year old brain is not fully developed and impulse control is not fully functioning until at least 25 years old, but that could be another book.

There has been a lot of press about sexual assault on college campuses lately. My best advice is to not put yourself in that position. This goes for boys and girls alike. Often alcohol is involved so have a plan in place to not get into a compromising position at, or, after parties. Again, the buddy system is very helpful here. If something does happen and you are the victim of assault you should either report it to campus police or go to the health center. Please be aware of your surroundings and be safe. Use the blue lights if you need to and call security if you are afraid to walk back to your dorm alone at night.

Resources

You will have lots of resources once you get to campus. Make sure you take advantage of the ones that you need. You made it this far and you will be fine in college though it is normal to be a little homesick or miss your friends. If you are really struggling you should go to the counseling office and make an appointment to speak with a counselor. Many, many other students are having the same feelings that you are so don't be afraid to talk it out with a professional.

Office Hours

I would be very remiss to write a handbook on all things college and not mention office hours. You will probably hear about these at orientation and you most likely heard about them at every single college tour you attended. Office hours are time set aside by professors to be available for students. You can just drop in if you have a quick question or make an appointment for something that might take more time. I've even heard that some students drop by just to chat with their professors!

Now that you're ready to take the big step to being a college freshman, go out there any make the most of it!

1. Is making friends hard?
2. What if I get lost on campus?
3. What if I don't want to party? Will people think I'm strange?
4. What happens if I don't really like the new friends that I make?

www.ingramcontent.com/pod-product-compliance
Lightning Source LLC
LaVergne TN
LVHW051522070426
835507LV00023B/3249